CROCHETED WIRE JEWELRY

INNOVATIVE DESIGNS & PROJECTS BY LEADING ARTISTS

CROCHETED WIRE JEWELRY

INNOVATIVE DESIGNS & PROJECTS BY LEADING ARTISTS

Arline M. Fisch

 LARK BOOKS

A Division of Sterling Publishing Co., Inc. • New York / London

The Library of Congress has cataloged the hardcover edition as follows:

Crocheted wire jewelry : innovative designs & projects by leading artists / [compiled by] Arline M. Fisch.
   p. cm.
  Includes bibliographical references and index.
  ISBN 1-57990-660-5 (hardcover)
  1. Jewelry making. 2. Wire craft. I. Fisch, Arline M.
 TT212.C76 2006
 745.594'2--dc22

                  2005024696

10 9 8 7 6 5 4 3 2 1

Published by Lark Books, A Division of
Sterling Publishing Co., Inc.
387 Park Avenue South, New York, NY 10016

First Paperback Edition 2009
Text © 2006, Arline M. Fisch
Photography © 2006, Lark Books unless otherwise specified
Illustrations © 2006, Lark Books

Distributed in Canada by Sterling Publishing,
c/o Canadian Manda Group, 165 Dufferin Street
Toronto, Ontario, Canada M6K 3H6

Distributed in the United Kingdom by GMC Distribution Services,
Castle Place, 166 High Street, Lewes, East Sussex, England BN7 1XU

Distributed in Australia by Capricorn Link (Australia) Pty Ltd.,
P.O. Box 704, Windsor, NSW 2756 Australia

The written instructions, photographs, designs, patterns, and projects in this volume are intended for the personal use of the reader and may be reproduced for that purpose only. Any other use, especially commercial use, is forbidden under law without written permission of the copyright holder.

Every effort has been made to ensure that all the information in this book is accurate. However, due to differing conditions, tools, and individual skills, the publisher cannot be responsible for any injuries, losses, and other damages that may result from the use of the information in this book.

If you have questions or comments about this book, please contact:
Lark Books
67 Broadway
Asheville, NC 28801
(828) 253-0467

Manufactured in China

ISBN 13: 978-1-57990-660-3 (hardcover) 978-1-60059-481-6 (paperback)

For information about custom editions, special sales, and premium and corporate purchases, please contact Sterling Special Sales Department at 800-805-5489 or specialsales@sterlingpub.com.

DEVELOPMENT EDITOR:
Marthe Le Van

EDITOR:
Donna Druchunas

ART DIRECTOR:
828, Inc.

ART DIRECTOR, PHOTOGRAPHY:
Susan McBride

COVER DESIGNER:
Barbara Zaretsky

ASSOCIATE EDITOR:
Nathalie Mornu

ASSOCIATE ART DIRECTOR:
Shannon Yokeley

EDITORIAL ASSISTANCE:
Delores Gosnell

EDITORIAL INTERN:
David Squires

PHOTOGRAPHER:
keithwright.com

ILLUSTRATOR:
Orrin Lundgren

PROOFREADER:
Karen Levy

contents

INTRODUCTION   6

THE BASICS
Characteristics of Wire   8
Tools   11
Findings   13
Crochet Essentials   14
Basic Crochet Stitches   16

THE PROJECTS   31
Chain Stitch Projects
Purple Haze Necklace
Arline M. Fisch   32

Multicolored Bracelets
Inger Blix Kvammen   34

Cube Pendant
Eugenie Keefer Bell   36

Fluffy Silver Necklace
Inger Blix Kvammen   38

Single Crochet Projects
Two Layer Pendant
Arline M. Fisch   41

Rosette Earrings
Hanne Behrens   44

Silver Discs Necklace
Arline M. Fisch   46

Three-Disc Lariat
Arline M. Fisch   48

Bead Earrings
Anastacia Pesce   51

Five Stitch Chain
Anastacia Pesce   54

Pinwheel Brooch
Tina Fung Holder   56

Gourd Pendant
Anastacia Pesce   58

Sphere Necklace
Anne Mondro   61

Calla Pendant
Annegret Schmid   64

Crochet Projects with Beads
Silver & Hematite Beaded Necklace
Arline M. Fisch   68

Round Spiral Brooch
Arline M. Fisch   70

Crochet Necklace
Lilo Sermol   73

Found Object Necklace
Bonnie Meltzer   76

Amber & Crystal Bracelet
Zuzana Rudavska   78

Flourish Scarf
Kathryn Harris   80

**Double Crochet & Crochet
Pattern Projects**
Lilacs Spiral Necklace
Kandy Hawley   84

Eel Trap Necklace
Hanne Behrens   86

Elizabethan Partlet
Jesse Mathes   90

Hairpin Lace Projects
Bangle Bracelets
Arline M. Fisch   93

Hairpin Lace Choker
Arline M. Fisch   96

Hairpin Lace Necklace
Arline M. Fisch   98

Hairpin Lace Collar
Arline M. Fisch   100

**Projects Using Other
Crochet Methods**
Corn Necklace
Joan Dulla   102

Yellow Gold Necklace
Michael David Sturlin   105

THE GALLERY   108
GLOSSARY   118
CONTRIBUTING ARTISTS   120
ARTIST INDEX   126
INDEX   127
ACKNOWLEDGMENTS   128
ABOUT THE AUTHOR   128
NOTES ON SUPPLIERS   128

introduction

Today, crochet is gaining a popularity that it hasn't seen since the 1960s and '70s. This simple technique is ideal for making jewelry. With a few basic stitches, you can quickly create both flat and three-dimensional forms that are lightweight yet range from open linear constructions to densely layered and patterned surfaces. By adding small glass and stone beads or pearls, you can create jewelry with a great richness of surface textures and colors. Crocheting with wire allows you to create a lacy structure that holds its form while retaining a great deal of flexibility, and it is no more difficult than working with yarn.

Crochet has an enormous range of scales, patterns, materials, and styles. It can be delicate and dainty when done in small gauge materials, or it can be massive and heavy when materials are multiplied. Extremely simple pieces can be made using only chain stitch, and highly complex pieces can be made using pattern stitches. It can be a very loose and open structure if large hooks are used, or it can be a completely dense surface when small hooks are used to make tight stitches. An exciting aspect of crochet is its improvisational character—its ability to grow in any direction. A hook can be inserted into any opening and loops developed from that point, while the path of stitches can be totally random, allowing forms to evolve freely.

For the textile artist who wants to make jewelry, it is an easy transition from working with yarn to working with metal, because it only involves an adjustment in tension to suit a material with different properties and characteristics. For the artist used to working with metal, it requires a new mindset—there is no opportunity to file away inconsistencies or correct surfaces. Crochet does not make sharp edges or shiny surfaces. Instead, it offers freedom of line and softer form, along with transparency and texture, but it does require learning the basics of crochet, including how to control the sequence of stitches to arrive at the desired result.

Learning a new technique is a bit more difficult than adapting to a new material, but a number of artists have taken up the challenge and developed innovative variations that work well in metal. Eugenie Keefer Bell's random but dense layering of chain and slip stitch (page 36) contrasts sharply with Inger Blix Kvammen's fluffy chain stitch necklace (page 38), while Michael David Sturlin has perfected an unusual method for producing almost solid tubes of single loops (page 105).

In my own case, I found that chain stitch was quite easy to make in a variety of gauges of wire using medium to large crochet hooks. I made miles of chain stitch and configured the chains in different ways to make dramatic necklaces (pages 32 and 68). I also found hairpin lace quite easy to crochet, and made endless lengths to assemble into various jewelry forms (bracelets on page 93 and necklaces on pages 96–100). It was only after making several projects with these easy techniques that I became brave enough to try using smaller crochet hooks to make more complicated shapes, such as discs and spheres. After some practice, I also started adapting medallion and lace patterns to a larger scale for collars and neck pieces.

Crochet is an interlooped structure of repetitive stitches made with a single hook. In fact, it gets its name from the French word for hook, *crochet*. Surprisingly, there is no evidence of crochet in Europe before 1800, although knitting and many other textile structures have a very long history. Crochet seems to have made its earliest appearance in northern Europe in the form of warm clothing made from wool using slip stitch. Found in Norway and Scotland, this is sometimes called "shepherds' knitting" even though it is produced with a single hook.

Some textile historians believe that crochet was first developed as a way of imitating traditional lace designs, but in a quicker and more efficient manner. The earliest known crochet used tiny hooks and very fine cotton thread to make a kind of poor-man's lace in the same patterns but with less delicacy. Hairpin lace crochet was invented in 1856 to imitate delicate needle laces applied to a net background.

Crochet became a polite pastime in nineteenth-century drawing rooms, where ladies made lace to trim household linens and undergarments. But it also accompanied American pioneer women as both a form of entertainment and a way of producing simple, warm clothing. During the Depression of the 1930s, women made lace collars and cuffs and accessories such as purses and gloves to extend and enhance their wardrobes. There were many patterns, simple and complex, published for the skilled and fashion-conscious homemaker. In the late '40s, after World War II, the focus changed again to household items such as afghans, tablecloths, and lace doilies, which were made as much for entertainment as for function.

In the late '60s, crochet exploded in popularity as artists explored the technique for sculptural purposes, working in unusual and large-scale materials. That particular aspect has since diminished, but there is now a lively revival of interest in crochet as a means of personal expression through both home decor objects and fashion. Over the past ten years, crochet has developed a new and exciting direction as many hobbyists and artists have begun using wire to create exciting jewelry designs.

Because I found it challenging to follow standard crochet patterns, I have written the instructions for the projects in this book in an easy-to-follow format without abbreviations. I hope the projects presented by various artists will provide you with the initial skills and experience to become comfortable crocheting with wire. After learning the basic stitches and making a few of the projects, you will find that you can easily improvise your own three-dimensional forms. Images of crocheted jewelry designs by contemporary artists spread throughout the book will inspire you to create your own designs. There are so many possibilities!

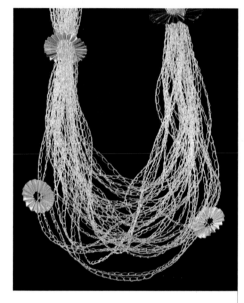

^ **ARLINE M. FISCH**
Linear Madness, 1996
Dimensions vary. Fine silver wire, sterling rosettes; chain stitched, wrapped, fastened
Photo © William Gullette

the basics

WIRE GAUGES & METRIC EQUIVALENTS

Browne & Sharpe	Metric
12 gauge	2.05 mm
14 gauge	1.62 mm
16 gauge	1.29 mm
18 gauge	1.01 mm
20 gauge	0.81 mm
22 gauge	0.63 mm
24 gauge	0.51 mm
26 gauge	0.40 mm
28 gauge	0.33 mm
30 gauge	0.25 mm
32 gauge	0.20 mm
34 gauge	0.15 mm

CHARACTERISTICS OF WIRE

Wire is a single, flexible strand of metal, usually round in cross section. Wires in copper, brass, silver, gold, and soft iron are ideal for crochet, and are available in a range of sizes appropriate for crochet. Wires are measured in gauges or in millimeters. In the United States, the Browne & Sharpe Gauge is used for nonferrous metals. In this system, the larger the gauge number, the finer the wire. The millimeter system uses actual diameter measurements so the larger the number, the larger the wire.

I don't recommend using anything heavier than 24 gauge (0.51 mm) for crochet, because it is too difficult to work with. To create the appearance of a wire with a larger diameter, use multiple strands of the thinner gauge wires (28 to 34 gauge, 0.33 to 0.15 mm). It is possible to work with heavier wires such as 20 gauge (0.81 mm), if your hands can manage the extra strain. Heavier wires are more commonly used for making clasps and other findings.

Wire itself does not stretch, but crochet structures made with wire can be stretched with your hands, providing the crochet has been made loosely. It is very difficult (and not advisable) to undo crochet with wire because the wire is not elastic. Once the loops are formed, they tend to lock around each other, making it almost impossible to pull them out. The loops actually bend the wire, so it is not easy to unravel a crochet chain without creating kinks that can damage or break the strand. The wires used in this book are all quite soft in their initial state. However, like all metal, wire tends to work harden as it is manipulated, so it is always best to use fresh wire directly from a spool.

Copper Wire

Commercial copper wire is extremely soft and malleable and is readily available in many thin gauges. It is important to purchase copper wire on spools rather than in small coils.

Uncoated wire will darken with handling and exposure to air, but it can also be deliberately colored with heat or chemical patinas after crocheting.

Coated copper wires have a thin covering of nylon or polyester resin that is dyed to produce a wide range of colors. Originally intended for industrial and electronic purposes, coated copper wire is now being marketed to craft artists and is readily available at bead shops, from craft suppliers, and on the Internet.

Some colored wire is silver plated, then coated and dyed, making it slightly stiffer. Silver-plated wire does have vibrant and intense colors, but it is more costly than coated copper, and it tends to be sold in craft shops on very small spools of 15 yards (13.7 m). These small spools are only useful for accents. Silver-plated copper wire is, however, available in larger quantities on the Internet.

Coated copper wire is packaged on spools in different quantities, and the length varies with the gauge. The regular spools sold over the counter in bead shops range from 20 to 125 yards (18.2 to 113.8 m), depending upon the gauge. Larger spools with 1/4 pound (114 g) of wire are readily available on the Internet, while larger quantities can be found at surplus outlets or special ordered from some manufacturers.

It is important to note that colors achieved with dyes are not always consistent from one spool to the next because of differences in dye lots. The color can also change if left in bright sunlight over long periods of time, so it is best to store the spools out of direct sunlight.

COPPER WIRE SPOOL SIZES

Wire Size	Spool Size(s)
12 gauge	50 feet per pound (454 g), sold only by the pound
14 gauge	80 feet per pound (454 g), sold only by the pound
16 gauge	125 feet per pound (454 g), sold only by the pound

Wire Size	Small Spool	Medium Spool	1/4 pound (114 g)	1 pound (454 g)
18 gauge	4 yards (3.6 m)	10 yards (9.1 m)	50 feet (15.2 m)	200 feet (60.9 m)
20 gauge	6 yards (5.5 m)	15 yards (13.7 m)	80 feet (24.3 m)	320 feet (97.5 m)
22 gauge	8 yards (7.3 m)	15 yards (13.7 m)	125 feet (38.1 m)	507 feet (154.5 m)
24 gauge	10 yards (9.1 m)	20 yards (18.2 m)	200 feet (60.9 m)	806 feet (245.7 m)
26 gauge	15 yards (13.7 m)	30 yards (27.4 m)	300 feet (91.4 m)	1276 feet (389 m)
28 gauge	15 yards (13.7 m)	40 yards (36.6 m)	500 feet (152.4 m)	2020 feet (615.7 m)
30 gauge	30 yards (27.4 m)	50 yards (45.7 m)	800 feet (243.8 m)	3205 feet (976.9 m)
32 gauge	30 yards (27.4 m)	100 yards (91.4 m)	1270 feet (387 m)	5086 feet (1550.2 m)
34 gauge	30 yards (27.4 m)	125 yards (114.3 m)	2009 feet (612.3 m)	8039 feet (2450.3 m)

Brass Wire

Brass is an alloy of copper and zinc and is therefore not as soft or malleable as copper. It also tends to work harden more quickly. It can be found on small spools in bead and craft shops, and it can also be ordered in larger quantities from wire suppliers on the Internet and from some jewelry suppliers.

Silver Wire

Sterling silver and fine silver wire are sold by the Troy ounce where 20 dwt (pennyweights) equals 1 ounce (31.1 g). It is also available on spools, in 24 to 32 gauge (0.51 to 0.20 mm). It is better to purchase silver wire by the ounce, rather than by the foot, because most crochet uses a large quantity of wire and it is helpful to have a continuous strand from start to finish. It is also important to purchase small-gauge wires on a spool rather than in a coil to avoid tangles when working.

Fine silver is an almost pure metal and is very soft. It does work harden as it is manipulated and must be annealed to use a second time. Sterling silver, an alloy of copper and silver, is stiffer than fine silver and is also a bit stronger. If reworked, it will need to be annealed and then pickled in an acid bath to restore its white color.

Gold Wire

Gold wire is available in a variety of alloys that determine its color and karat. The purest gold is 24-karat gold, which is a bit too soft to be self-supporting in a crochet structure, although it does work harden with use. Other options include 23-karat yellow gold, which is a warm, rich color and extremely malleable, and 18-karat yellow gold, which is stiffer but will produce a sturdy crochet structure even in very thin gauges. White and green gold tend to be harder than yellow gold at the same karat and gauge. It is preferable to buy the wire on spools in the exact gauge required, and to order it in an annealed temper. Gold wire is sold by the Troy ounce where 20 dwt (pennyweights) equals 1 ounce (31.1 g).

Gold-filled wire has a thin layer of karat gold (usually 14 karat) heat and pressure bonded to a base of brass, which gives a gold surface at a much lower cost. It is referred to as 14/20 to indicate that the

gold layer is $\frac{1}{20}$th of the thickness of the wire or about 5 percent of the total weight. The wire should be ordered in an annealed state, also known as dead soft, which will handle like sterling silver. It is important not to scratch or damage the gold surface to avoid future tarnishing.

Gold plating is an electrolytic process, which puts a very thin layer of gold over other metals and is usually done to an already completed project. Gold-plating solutions are extremely hazardous, so it is best to have this process done by a commercial plater.

Other Metals

Other metals that can be crocheted are stainless steel, soft iron wire (sometimes called stove wire), and niobium. The latter is a refractory metal that can be colored by heat or in an electrolytic bath after it has been crocheted. It can also be purchased already colored from a few sources, but it is preferable to work the raw metal and color it afterward to avoid surface scratches. Aluminum is not well suited to crochet because it work hardens quickly and breaks easily with very little stress.

TOOLS

Crochet hooks are the basic tools, and an assortment of sizes will be required for the projects in this book. Crochet hooks are made in a variety of materials, but for working with wire it is advisable to use those made of steel or anodized aluminum so the hook will not be damaged by the constant friction of the metal wire. There are many brands of hooks currently on the market, including some with ergonomically designed handles.

FIGURE 1

The basic shape and length of crochet hooks is fairly standard (figure 1). The diameter of the shaft, rather than the hook at the tip, determines the size. There are several different numbering systems for crochet hook sizes, depending upon the material and the manufacturer. The metric system is the only constant measurement scale and is now often included along with the size indicator on each hook.

Cleaning Silver Wire Jewelry

To clean and remove tarnish from silver wire constructions without acid or harsh chemicals, use the following method:

 Line a glass bowl with aluminum foil and fill with boiling water.

2 Add 2 tablespoons (15 ml) of baking soda to the water in the bowl.

3 Immerse the silver in the solution, making sure the silver is in direct contact with the foil. Allow it to soak for 30 to 60 seconds, or longer if necessary.

4 Remove the silver and rinse it in warm or cold tap water.

Steel Hooks

Steel crochet hooks are numbered from the largest, size 00 (3.50 mm), to the smallest, size 14 (0.75 mm). They are produced by several companies and the numbered sizes are not consistent. In most cases, the slight variations are not going to make a difference in the end result, but checking the metric size will give a totally accurate measurement. (Not all metric sizes have U.S. size equivalents.)

STEEL HOOK NUMERICAL SIZES & METRIC EQUIVALENTS

U.S. Size	Metric
00	3.50 mm
0	3.25 mm
1	2.75 mm
2	2.25 mm
3	2.10 mm
4	2.00 mm
5	1.90 mm
6	1.80 mm
7	1.65 mm
8	1.50 mm
9	1.40 mm
10	1.30 mm
11	1.10 mm
12	1.00 mm
13	0.85 mm
14	0.75 mm

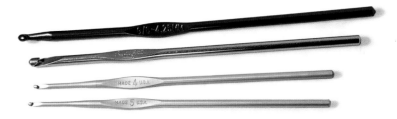

Yarn Hooks

Yarn crochet hooks are larger in size than steel hooks (although there is some overlap) and usually made of aluminum, plastic, wood, or bamboo. They use a letter designation from the smallest, size B (2.25 mm), to the largest, size Q (15.00 mm). Here, too, the metric equivalents for each letter vary somewhat from one manufacturer to another, so it is best to check the actual size when following a set of instructions.

YARN HOOK LETTER SIZES & METRIC EQUIVALENTS

U.S. Size	Metric
B	2.25 mm
C	2.75 mm
D	3.25 mm
E	3.50 mm
F	3.75 mm
G	4.00 mm
H	5.00 mm
I	5.50 mm
J	6.00 mm
K	6.50 mm
N	9.00 mm
P	10.00 mm
Q	15.00 mm

Hairpin Lace Frames

Hairpin lace frames come in a variety of styles and are available from yarn shops and online yarn catalogs. The most common are adjustable frames, which consist of two rods and two braces with multiple holes with settings to make the frame 1 to 4 inches (2.5 to 10.2 cm) wide. A more comfortable type of frame is a single size made of one U-shaped rod with a removable brace on the bottom, available in 1- to 3-inch (2.5 to 7.6 cm) widths. This type of frame can easily be constructed from a steel rod bent into a U shape, with a dowel stick used as a brace.

Long round-nose pliers   Small round-nose pliers   Needle-nose pliers   Wire cutters   Chain-nose pliers

Additional Tools
• Darning needles, for finishing ends
• Small sewing scissors, for cutting thin-gauge wires
• Small needle- or chain-nose pliers
• Small wire cutters
• Standard jeweler's tools, for finishing many of the projects
(See the Glossary on page 118 for a list of jeweler's tools with definitions.)

FINDINGS

Findings is the term used for jewelry fittings that attach the finished design to the body or clothing and make it wearable. These findings include clasps for necklaces and bracelets, pins and catches for brooches, bails or loops for pendants, and myriad earring hooks and clutches. Findings can be made by hand when a particular design and size is needed, or they can be purchased ready-made in a wide range of styles, sizes, and metals. Each project in this book indicates the findings specified by the artist, but many other alternatives are possible.

Magnetic clasp   Magnetic clasp   Sliding clasp   Ear Wire

Toggle clasp   S hook   Hook-and-eye clasp   Pin back

‹ JOAN DULLA
Touched, 2002
12 x 12 x 4 inches (30.5 x 30.5 x 10.2 cm)
Sterling silver wire, fine silver wire,
coated copper wire; crocheted
Photo © W. Scott Mitchell

CROCHET ESSENTIALS

Before you can start your first crochet project or practice crochet stitches, you must learn how to hold the hook and wire, and how to manipulate the wire as you form the stitches.

Holding the Hook & Wire

There are many ways to hold the hook and wire for crochet. The best method is to hold the hook in your right hand (if you are right-handed) while holding both the work and the wire in your left hand. Hold your left hand still while using your right hand to manipulate the hook by slipping it under the wire and drawing the wire through the existing loop to form the next stitch. It is important to hold the stitch to be entered between your thumb and middle finger, while using your index finger to adjust the tension of the wire. One technique is to wrap the wire around your left hand several times before holding it tightly against your index finger to maintain an even—but not tight—tension. Another method is to wrap the wire around only your index finger several times, but this may require protecting your finger with a leather thimble.

There are many other ways to hold the hook and manipulate the wire to form loops, especially for left-handers (see page 22). Some people prefer to wrap the wire around the hook for each stitch rather like knitting. It is best to try several approaches to find the one that is most comfortable and efficient, and produces the most consistent results.

Tension

When crocheting with wire, maintaining tension is essential for producing even stitches. This is the most difficult adjustment to make when changing from yarn to wire, but it is important to acquire the right balance in order to work comfortably. Each crocheter will find a unique way to do this, but the process must allow the wire to flow freely to make stitches that are consistent in size and large enough for the hook to enter and exit each loop. It is important not to pull the stitches or the wire too tightly or it will be impossible to insert the hook for subsequent stitches. At the same time, making loops that are consistent in size will give a better appearance to the finished structure.

Front & Back of Work

In crochet, the front, or right side, of the work is the side that will be worn facing out when the item is complete. The front is the part of the work that will be seen

< **INGER BLIX KVAMMEN**
Silver Fur with Gold Front, 2004
Width from neckline, 4¾ inches (12.1 cm)
Sterling silver wire, 18-karat gold wire; crocheted
Photo © artist

when the jewelry is worn. The back, or wrong side, is the side that will be hidden when the work is complete. The back may be the inside of a three-dimensional item or the side of a flat piece of jewelry that is worn facing the body.

Yarn Over Hook

Crochet stitches are made by wrapping wire around the hook and pulling it through loops. The process of wrapping the wire around the hook is called "yarn over hook." This is used in all crochet stitches. To perform yarn over hook, pass the hook under the wire and catch the wire in the notch of the hook.

Making a Slipknot

A slipknot attaches the wire to your crochet hook.

1. Make a loop in the wire, leaving a tail the length indicated in the project instructions.

2. Use the crochet hook to pull the wire through the loop, creating a new loop. Make sure you pull the wire attached to the spool, not the tail, through to create the new loop (figure 1).

3. Leave the new loop on the crochet hook, and gently tug the wires to tighten the slipknot.

Fastening Off

After completing the crochet stitches in a project, you must fasten off the wire so the crochet can't unravel.

1. Cut the wire, leaving a tail of wire the length specified in the project instructions.

2. Put the end of the tail through the last loop of the crochet.

3. Pull gently to tighten.

Repeating Stitches & Steps

In crochet, you frequently repeat the same steps several times within the same row or in successive rows. Sometimes the instructions will tell you which steps to repeat. At other times, the instructions will include a star (*). Further along in the step, you will find instructions that say "repeat from *." The instructions will tell you to repeat the stitches following the * either a specified number of times or until you reach the end of the row or round.

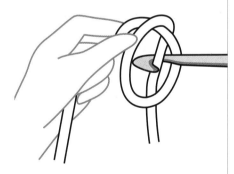

FIGURE 1

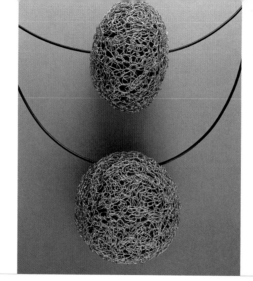

BASIC CROCHET STITCHES

All crochet is constructed from a small number of basic stitches. The stitches vary in height, allowing you to create designs that are densely packed with stitches as well as designs that are light and airy. The techniques for making the basic stitches vary slightly for right- and left-handed crocheters.

In the following sections, I recommend the type of wire and size of crochet hook to use for practice. It is also wise to make a small sample of each stitch before beginning a project, using the specific wire and hook size indicated in the project instructions.

Chain Stitch

Chain stitch is the basic stitch that is the foundation stitch for beginning almost all crochet structures. When instructions direct you to make a chain or to chain a specific number of stitches, always use this stitch. When instructions say "chain 15," this means to make a chain that is 15 stitches long.

MATERIALS & TOOLS

To practice, use 28-gauge (0.33 mm) wire with a 2-mm (size 4 U.S.) steel crochet hook.

STEP BY STEP

1. Make a slipknot at the end of the wire or simply pull the tail of the wire through a loop made 3 or 4 inches (7.6 or 10.2 cm) from its end.

2. Insert the hook into the slipknot or loop.

3. Pass the hook under the wire and catch the wire in the notch of the hook (figure 1).

4. Rotate the hook to the left and draw the wire through the loop, creating a new stitch (figure 2). Turning the hook to the left allows it to exit the loop upside down so it doesn't catch any other existing loops.

5. Repeat steps 3 and 4 to create a chain of any length (figure 3).

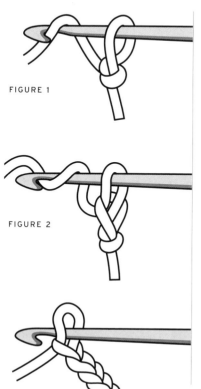

FIGURE 1

FIGURE 2

FIGURE 3

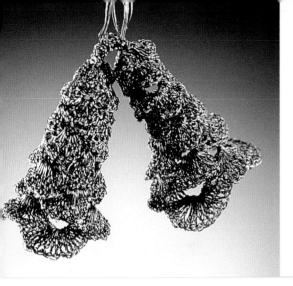

< ANNEGRET SCHMID
Untitled (detail), 1996
Length, 31½ inches (80 cm);
each flower, 2¼ x 1½ inches (5.7 x 3.8 cm)
Iron wire; crocheted
Photo © Lutz Hartmann

> ZUZANA RUDAVSKA
Double-sided Geometric Pendant I, 2001
2⅛ x 3½ x ⅜ inches (5.4 x 8.9 x 1 cm)
Gold-filled wire, sterling silver,
dyed freshwater pearls; crocheted
Photo © G. Erml

Stitch Smart

• *Each successive loop should slip easily through the previous one. If it doesn't, the tension on the wire is too tight and needs to be relaxed. Move your fingers closer to the stitch being made to gain more control over the tension.*

• *The size of each loop is determined by the shank rather than the tip of the hook, so as you crochet, slip each loop down onto the shank of the crochet hook to open the stitch, and do not allow it to tighten when it is slipped off the hook.*

• *The chain tends to twist as it is made. Untwist it with your fingers as you make additional rows. When using chain stitch by itself, you can stretch the chain by pulling gently, but it will always twist and curl. This characteristic creates a lively effect in wire. Hanging a weight, such as a glass, stone, or metal bead, on the bottom of the chain will minimize the curling.*

Double Chain Stitch

Double chain stitch will make a wider and sturdier foundation. It works especially well for creating button loops.

MATERIALS & TOOLS
To practice, use 28-gauge (0.33 mm) wire with a 2-mm (size 4 U.S.) steel crochet hook.

STEP BY STEP
1. Make a slipknot at the end of the wire or simply pull the tail of the wire through a loop made 3 or 4 inches (7.6 or 10.2 cm) from its end.

2. Make 2 chain stitches following steps 2 through 4 on page 16.

3. Insert the hook back into the first chain stitch.

4. Catch the wire and draw it through the chain to make a second loop on the hook.

5. Catch the wire again, and draw it through both loops on the hook.

6. Insert the hook under the left-hand loop of the 2 loops just slipped off the hook.

7. Catch the wire, turn the hook, and draw the wire through both loops on the hook.

8. Repeat steps 6 and 7 to create the desired length of double chain stitch.

‹ LILO SERMOL
Garland, 2003
8 ¾ x 5 ½ x 1 ½ inches (22.2 x 13.4 x 3.8 cm)
Coated copper wire; crocheted
Photo © artist

Slip Stitch

Slip stitch is an important basic stitch used for joining, shaping, and making a simple open structure.

MATERIALS & TOOLS

To practice, use 28-gauge (0.33 mm) wire with a 2-mm (size 4 U.S.) steel crochet hook.

STEP BY STEP

1. Make a foundation chain of the desired length.

2. Insert the hook into the second chain stitch from the hook (or the stitch specified in the project instructions).

3. Catch the wire and pull it through both the chain stitch and the loop on the hook all in one motion.

4. Insert the hook into the next chain and repeat step 3 for subsequent stitches (figure 1). Make 1 slip stitch in each stitch to crochet a row.

FIGURE 1

Single Crochet

Single crochet may be used in parallel rows, or in a circular or spiral sequence to make discs, spheres, and tubes. It creates a dense structure that can be plain or ribbed. It may also be used for joining or making a finished edge.

MATERIALS & TOOLS

To practice, use 28-gauge (0.33 mm) wire with a 2-mm (size 4 U.S.) steel crochet hook.

STEP BY STEP

1. Make a foundation chain of the desired length.

2. Insert the hook into the back loop of the second chain stitch from the hook (figure 2).

FIGURE 2

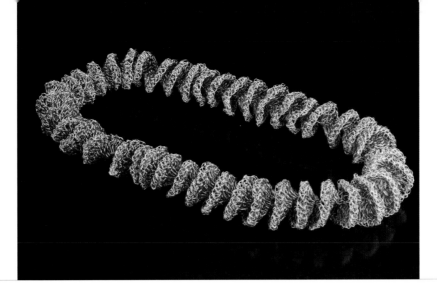

3. Pass the hook under the wire and turn the hook to the left to catch the wire (figure 3).

4. Draw the wire through the chain stitch, leaving 2 loops on the hook (figure 4).

5. Pass the hook under the wire again, turn the hook to catch the wire (figure 5).

6. Draw the wire through both loops on the hook to complete the stitch (figure 6).

7. Insert the hook into the next chain and repeat steps 3 through 6 for subsequent stitches. Make 1 single crochet in each stitch to crochet a row.

Stitch Smart

• *Working into the foundation chain is awkward. Be sure to hold the loop being worked on with the thumb and middle finger of your left hand to control the tension and the size of the loops.*

• *To make a second row of single crochet, add 1 chain stitch before turning to start the new row. This is called a "turning chain." Make 1 single crochet in each single crochet stitch across the row.*

• *To work single crochet in the round, forming a circle, join the end of the foundation chain with a slip stitch into the first loop, then add 1 chain stitch before beginning the first round. Add 1 chain stitch at the beginning of each new round.*

• *Unless directions specify otherwise, always insert the hook under both loops at the top of each stitch as you crochet additional rows.*

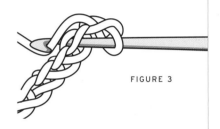

FIGURE 3

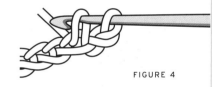

FIGURE 4

FIGURE 5

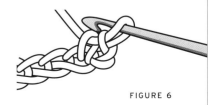

FIGURE 6

FIGURE 1

FIGURE 2

FIGURE 3

FIGURE 4

FIGURE 5

FIGURE 6

Double Crochet

Double crochet stitches have more height, resulting in rows that are farther apart, with a more open structure than single crochet. A double crochet stitch is actually two rows high but is made in a single passage.

MATERIALS & TOOLS

To practice, use 28-gauge (0.33 mm) wire with a 2-mm (size 4 U.S.) steel crochet hook.

STEP BY STEP

1. Make a foundation chain of the desired length.

2. Wrap the wire once around the hook (figure 1).

3. Insert the hook into the back loop of the fourth chain stitch from the hook (figure 2).

4. Catch the wire, turn the hook, and draw the wire through the stitch to create 3 loops on the hook (figure 3).

5. Catch the wire and draw it through the first 2 loops on the hook (figure 4).

6. Catch the wire again (figure 5) and draw it through the remaining 2 loops on the hook to complete the stitch (figure 6).

7. Repeat steps 2 through 6, inserting the hook into the next chain in step 3, to make the next stitch. Make 1 double crochet stitch in each stitch to crochet a row.

Stitch Smart

• *To make a second row of double crochet, add 3 chain stitches before turning to start the new row. Make 1 double crochet in each double crochet stitch across the row, inserting the hook under both loops in each stitch of the previous row.*

• *Always add 3 chain stitches before beginning each new row. Failure to do this causes drastic shrinking of the edges. When crocheting in the round, it is also necessary to add 3 chain stitches before beginning each new round.*

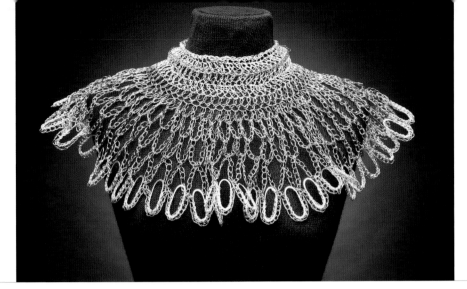

‹ ARLINE M. FISCH
Lacy Net, 2001
8 x 19 inches (20.3 x 48.3 cm)
Fine silver wire, coated copper wire,
sterling silver; crocheted, forged
Photo © William Gullette

Half Double Crochet

Half double crochet is a shortened version of double crochet and forms a space halfway between the single and the double crochet rows. It is not as widely used as single and double crochet, but it can be quite useful as an intermediary step when developing a gradual transition from one pattern stitch to another.

MATERIALS & TOOLS

To practice, use 28-gauge (0.33 mm) wire with a 2-mm (size 4 U.S.) steel crochet hook.

STEP BY STEP

1. Make a foundation chain of the desired length.

2. Wrap the wire once around the hook (figure 7).

3. Insert the hook into the third chain stitch from the hook.

4. Catch the wire and draw a loop through the chain, leaving 3 loops on the hook (figure 8).

5. Catch the wire and draw it through all 3 loops on the hook to complete the stitch (figure 9).

6. Repeat steps 2 through 5, inserting the hook into the next chain in step 3, to make the next stitch. Make 1 half double crochet stitch in each stitch to crochet a row.

FIGURE 7

FIGURE 8

FIGURE 9

> ### Stitch Smart
> • *To make a second row of half double crochet, add 2 chain stitches before turning to start the new row. Make 1 half double crochet in each half double crochet stitch across the row.*
>
> • *The hook can be inserted under both loops or under only the back or front loop, but be consistent across the row. This applies to all other crochet stitches as well.*

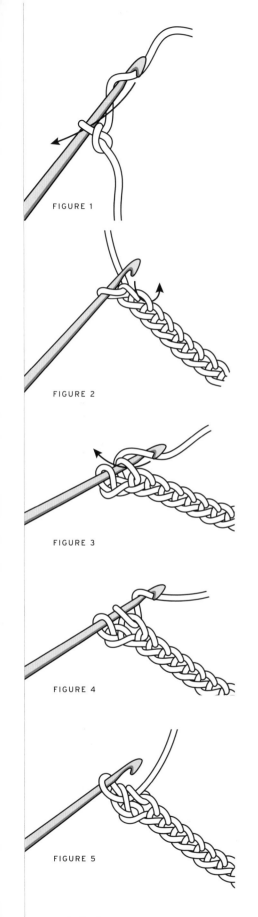

FIGURE 1

FIGURE 2

FIGURE 3

FIGURE 4

FIGURE 5

^ ARLINE M. FISCH
Seven Crochet Beads, 2003
3 x 12 inches (7.6 x 30.5 cm)
Fine silver wire, coated copper wire, sterling
silver spacers; crocheted, fabricated
Photo © artist

Left-Handed Crochet

Left-handed crochet requires an adjustment in the way the hook is held and manipulated to create stitches. Once this is made, most instructions can easily be followed.

Left-Handed Chain Stitch

MATERIALS & TOOLS

To practice, use 28-gauge (0.33 mm) wire with a 2-mm (size 4 U.S.) steel crochet hook.

STEP BY STEP

1. Hold the hook in your left hand with the work and wire in your right hand. The right hand remains still while the work is done with the left hand.

2. Make a slipknot at the end of the wire or simply pull the tail of the wire through a loop made 3 or 4 inches (7.6 or 10.2 cm) from its end.

3. Insert the hook into the slipknot or loop.

4. Pass the hook under the wire and catch the wire in the notch of the hook.

5. Rotate the hook to the right and draw the wire through the loop, as shown in figure 1, creating a new stitch. (Turning the hook to the right allows it to exit the loop upside down so it doesn't catch any other existing loops.)

6. Repeat steps 4 and 5 to create a series of chain stitches.

Left-Handed Single Crochet

MATERIALS & TOOLS

To practice, use 28-gauge (0.33 mm) wire with a 2-mm (size 4 U.S.) steel crochet hook.

STEP BY STEP

1. Make a foundation chain of the desired length.

2. Insert the hook into the back loop of the second chain stitch from the hook (figure 2).

3. Pass the hook under the wire and turn the hook to the right to catch the wire (figure 3).

4. Draw the wire through the chain stitch, leaving 2 loops on the hook (figure 4).

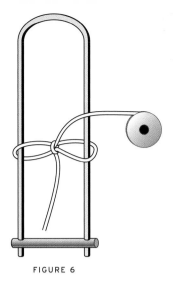

FIGURE 6

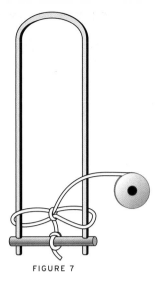

FIGURE 7

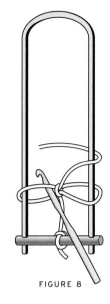

FIGURE 8

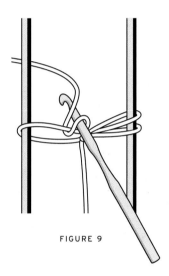

FIGURE 9

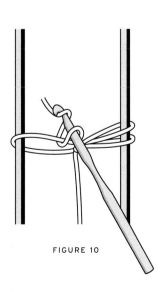

FIGURE 10

5. Pass the hook under the wire again, turn the hook to catch the wire, and draw the wire through both loops to complete the stitch (figure 5).

6. Insert the hook into the next chain and repeat steps 3 through 5 for subsequent stitches. Make 1 single crochet in each stitch to crochet a row.

> ### Stitch Smart
> • *All left-handed crochet stitches are made by passing the hook to the right and under the wire, instead of to the left as instructed in the basic crochet stitch instructions.*

Hairpin Lace

Hairpin lace is a form of crochet that is very well suited to working with wire. It is made on a strong U-shaped frame with a brace across the bottom. The wire is looped around the two parallel arms of the frame with a series of single crochet stitches worked in the center between the two arms. The size of the center is determined by the size of the crochet hook; the length of the loops is governed by the width of the frame. The technique produces light and open strips that can be used singly or combined in various ways to produce larger structures.

MATERIALS & TOOLS
To practice, use 28-gauge (0.33 mm) wire with a 3.5-mm (size 00 U.S.) steel crochet hook and a 1-inch-wide (2.5 cm) hairpin lace frame.

STEP BY STEP
1. Loop the wire around the frame and tie it in the center to create 2 loops with a knot in the middle (figure 6). Leave a wire tail of 6 to 8 inches (15.2 to 20.3 cm).

2. Tie the wire tail around the brace to anchor the structure at the bottom of the hairpin lace frame (figure 7).

3. Wrap the spool end of the wire around the right side of the frame and insert the hook into the left-hand loop (figure 8). Catch the wire, and draw the wire through, making a loop on the hook (figure 9), then make a chain stitch into the loop on the hook (figure 10).

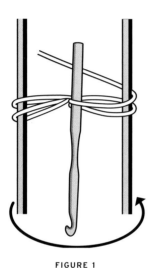

FIGURE 1

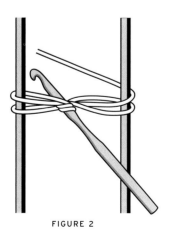

FIGURE 2

4. Flip the hook and turn the frame to the right, as shown in figure 1, creating a loop on the right-hand arm.

5. Insert the hook under the entire left-hand loop, as shown in figure 2. Draw the wire through to create a second loop on the hook. Yarn over hook, and complete a single crochet by drawing the wire through both loops.

6. Repeat steps 4 and 5, always turning the frame in the same direction and always inserting the hook under both parts of the left-hand loop.

Stitch Smart

• *To make a longer strip, remove the brace and slip the completed loops off the bottom of the frame. Replace the brace and continue the sequence for making hairpin lace.*

• *To finish hairpin lace, cut the wire, leaving a 6- to 8-inch (15.2 to 20.3 cm) tail, and draw the tail completely through the last crochet loop on the hook to fasten off.*

• *Caution: Do not pull or stretch the completed strip of hairpin lace, because this will damage the loops.*

• *It is necessary to give additional support to the completed strips either by crocheting into the loops to form an edge or by joining multiple strips together to make a larger structure.*

• *The scale of a piece of hairpin lace can be greatly increased by using multiple wires. The number of wires and their gauges will determine the size of the frame and the crochet hook. There is quite a bit of latitude in choice of wire, hook, and frame, but the relationship among all three elements must be considered carefully with respect to the finished project.*

Additional Techniques

Working Crochet in Rows

Crochet is most often worked back and forth in rows. At the end of each row, you normally chain 1 or more stitches before turning around. Specific instructions are included in the step-by-step section of each project.

The way you insert the hook into each stitch as you crochet a row changes the shape of the stitches and the texture of the resulting crocheted piece.

• Insert the hook under both sides of the loop in the previous row to form standard crochet stitches. Use this technique unless the project instructions specify otherwise.

• Insert the hook under only the back loop of each stitch to produce a subtle rib effect.

• Insert the hook under only the front loop of each stitch to produce a slight surface variation.

Working Crochet in Rounds

Crochet can also be worked circularly, or "in the round." There are two ways to work crochet in the round: in circular rounds, each round is made on top of the previous round and joined with a slip stitch at the end to form a circle. In spiral rounds, each round continues from the previous round without a join. Specific instructions are included in the step-by-step section of each project that is worked in rounds.

• To begin working in the round, form a foundation chain into a circle by making a slip stitch into the first loop, as shown in figures 3 and 4, or form a small circle of wire by wrapping it twice around a finger or the shaft of the crochet hook.

FIGURE 3

FIGURE 4

‹ JOAN DULLA
Pear, 2004
10 x 6 x 6 inches (25.4 x 15.2 x 15.2 cm)
Brass wire, copper wire; crocheted
Photo © W. Scott Mitchell

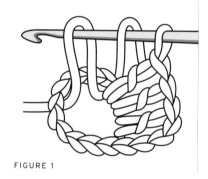

FIGURE 1

• To work circular crochet in joined rounds, begin each round with chains as specified in the pattern, and end each round with a slip stitch to join the last stitch of the round to the first. Figure 1 shows the first few stitches in a round of double crochet, beginning with 3 chains.

• To work circular crochet in a spiral, simply continue making stitches from one round to the next. Do not make any chain or slip stitches to start or end the rounds.

• Discs, domes, and other round crochet shapes begin with a small foundation chain joined to form a ring. The first row usually consists of multiple stitches in each loop of the chain or into the center of the circle of wire to enlarge the ring. The second and third rows further increase the number of stitches by making 2 stitches in each of those in the previous row. Subsequent rows may also increase stitches but at a slower rate, depending upon the intended result. Flat disc shapes require periodic increases to remain flat, while domed shapes may not require any additional stitches.

Crocheting with Beads

Any basic crochet stitch can be made with beads. Thread the beads onto the wire in advance. As each stitch is made, pull a bead up so it sits between the stitches. The beads tend to sit more firmly on the wrong side (back) of a structure, so it may need to be turned over when completed.

Adding a Bead in Chain Stitch

MATERIALS & TOOLS
To practice, use 28-gauge (0.33 mm) wire with a 2-mm (size 4 U.S.) steel crochet hook. Any beads that can be threaded onto the wire are suitable.

STEP BY STEP

1. Make 1 chain stitch.

2. Slide a bead up to the hook, and make the next chain. Add the beads at distances indicated in the project instructions.

> BONNIE MELTZER
Untitled, 2004
21¾ x 21¾ inches
(55.2 x 55.2 cm)
Copper wire, beads; crocheted
Photo © Patrick Smith

Adding a Bead in Single Crochet

MATERIALS & TOOLS

To practice, use 28-gauge (0.33 mm) wire with a 2-mm (size 4 U.S.) steel crochet hook. Any beads that can be threaded onto the wire are suitable.

STEP BY STEP

1. Insert the hook into the next stitch and bring a bead up to the hook.

2. Keeping the bead at the back of the work, yarn over and pull the strand through the stitch, yarn over and pull the strand through 2 loops on the hook.

Increasing

Increasing widens the crochet piece by adding more stitches. To increase, make 2 stitches into the next stitch as directed in the project instructions.

Decreasing

Decreasing narrows the crochet piece by eliminating some of the stitches. There are several ways to decrease. The specific techniques to use in each project are indicated in the instructions.

The easiest way to decrease is to skip a stitch. For example, skip 1 stitch, then make 1 single crochet in the second stitch from the crochet hook. This method is most often used at the beginning of a row, but it is also sometimes used in the middle of a row. This type of decrease leaves a small hole when worked in the middle of a row.

To decrease without leaving a hole, work 2 stitches together as follows: Draw a loop of wire through each of the next 2 stitches, yarn over hook, draw a loop through all 3 loops on the hook. You have decreased 1 stitch.

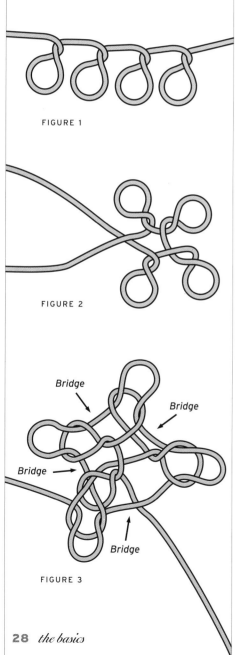

FIGURE 1

FIGURE 2

Bridge

Bridge

Bridge

Bridge

FIGURE 3

Joan Dulla's Crochet Technique

This method is used in the *Corn Necklace* on page 102. It will take time and practice to make even loops and to establish a comfortable working rhythm. It is best to make several trial beads with coated copper wire before attempting to work in fine silver or 18-karat gold.

MATERIALS & TOOLS

To practice, use 28-gauge (0.33 mm) wire with a 2-mm (size 4 U.S.) steel crochet hook.

STEP BY STEP

1. Form a loop around the shank of the crochet hook and spin the hook 1½ times to close the loop.

2. Make 3 more loops (figure 1) as in step 1 to form a four-leaf-clover shape, as shown in figure 2.

3. Round 1: Insert the crochet hook through the front of one of the loops made in step 2. Catch the wire with the hook and pull a new loop through. Push the wire up onto the shank of the crochet hook to open up the loop and to create stitches of a uniform shape and size.

4. Remove the crochet hook completely and place it into the next loop. Create another stitch as in step 3. Continue making new stitches, working in a clockwise direction, to make a new round of 4 loops.

5. Round 2: Make another round of stitches as in step 4, but at the same time, add 1 new stitch after each existing stitch by inserting the crochet hook under the wire bridge between the loops of the previous row (see figure 3) and pulling the wire through to create a new stitch. After completing this round, you have 8 stitches.

Michael David Sturlin's Crochet Technique

This technique, which is sometimes called Viking knitting, is used in the *Yellow Gold Necklace* on page 105. The stitches are made by forming wire loops with your fingers, and then tightening them on the shank of a knitting needle or awl.

MATERIALS & TOOLS

To practice, use two 20-inch (50.8 cm) pieces of 26-gauge (0.40 mm) wire and a 2.00-mm (size 0 U.S.) knitting needle or an awl of similar size.

STEP BY STEP

1. Wrap the wire around the tip of the knitting needle to form an oval, as shown in figure 4. Repeat this process to form a coil of 7 ovals (figure 5).

2. Hold one end of the coil in your fingers, and insert the tip of the needle through the other end of the coil. As shown in figure 6, turn the needle to twist the coil into a bundle, and then wrap wire around the bundle (figure 7).

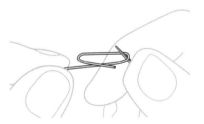

FIGURE 4

FIGURE 5

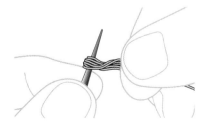

FIGURE 6

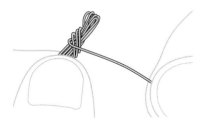

FIGURE 7

3. On one side of the wrapped wire, evenly spread apart the loops to create a base for the crochet (figure 1).

4. Thread the end of the wire through 2 adjoining loops, as shown in figure 2.

5. Pull the loop closed.

6. Tighten the loop carefully around the needle (figure 3).

7. Continue in a counterclockwise direction, making one loop at a time, until 1 inch (2.5 cm) of wire remains.

8. To add the next length of wire, insert the end of the new piece of wire into the next loop (figure 4) and splice it with the end of the old wire by twisting the ends together several times (figure 5). Leave the spliced end inside the tube and continue making stitches with the new length of wire.

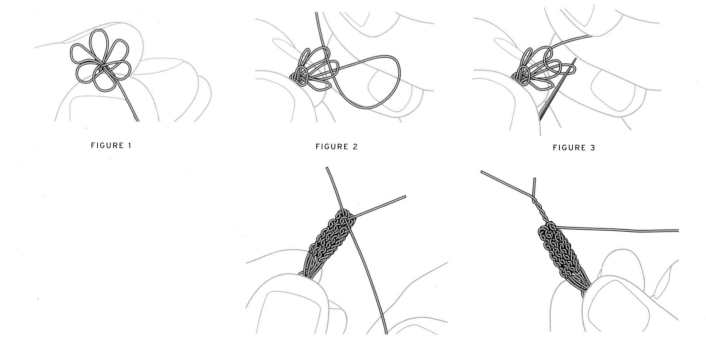

FIGURE 1

FIGURE 2

FIGURE 3

FIGURE 4

FIGURE 5

the projects

Sixteen talented artists have designed a wide range
of exciting projects as an introduction to crocheting
with wire. Try any or all of them to create
wonderful pieces of jewelry.

*purple
haze
necklace*

ARLINE M. FISCH

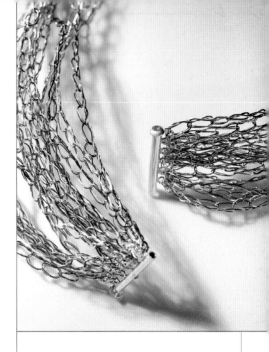

This elegant yet understated necklace is made from 16 separate lengths of chain stitch. After the chains are crocheted, the ends are threaded into the rings of a sterling silver sliding catch.

STEP BY STEP

Note: Start each chain with a slipknot, leaving a 6-inch (15.2 cm) tail. After each chain is complete, cut the wire, leaving a 6-inch (15.2 cm) tail, and pull the tail through the last loop to fasten off.

 With fine silver and 26-gauge purple wire held together and using the 5.00-mm yarn crochet hook, crochet 4 chains:

15 inches (38.1 cm)
16 inches (40.6 cm)
16¹⁄₂ inches (41.9 cm)
24 inches (61 cm)

2 With fine silver and 28-gauge purple wire held together and using the 5.00-mm yarn crochet hook, crochet 4 chains:

17 inches (43.2 cm)
18 inches (45.7 cm)
22 inches (55.9 cm)
27 inches (68.6 cm)

3 With fine silver and 28-gauge plum wire held together and using the 5.00-mm yarn crochet hook, crochet 8 chains:

15¹⁄₂ inches (39.4 cm)
20 inches (50.8 cm)
21 inches (53.3 cm)
23 inches (58.4 cm)
25 inches (63.5 cm)
29 inches (73.7 cm)
30 inches (76.2 cm), make 2

Finishing

4 Using the 6-inch (15.2 cm) tail at each end of the chains, thread the chains in order of size into the loops on the sliding catch.

5 Wrap each wire end through the loop several times, then clip off the excess wire with wire cutters.

6 If desired, use a small soldering torch to bead the cut end of the fine silver wire. Bury the ends of the copper wire in the wrapped coils.

PROJECT DIMENSIONS

8 inches wide x 11 inches long (20.3 x 27.9 cm), with a 5-inch (12.7 cm) inner diameter

MATERIALS

Fine silver wire, 26 gauge (0.4 mm), 1¹⁄₂ ounces (46.7 g)

Coated copper wire, purple, 26 gauge (0.4 mm), 1 spool, 30 yards (27.4 m)

Coated copper wire, purple, 28 gauge (0.33 m), 1 spool, 40 yards (36.6 m)

Coated copper wire, plum, 28 gauge (0.33 m), 1 spool, 40 yards (36.6 m)

Sterling silver sliding catch, 5 strand

TOOLS

Yarn crochet hook, 5.00 mm (size H U.S)

Wire cutters

Small soldering torch (optional)

Striker (optional)

Heat-resistant soldering surface (optional)

multicolored bracelets

INGER BLIX KVAMMEN

These multicolored bracelets feature a densely packed mass of chain stitch crocheted with groups of wires. The strands are tightly compressed into a form that fits closely around the wrist, and they can be left loose, or twisted to form a spiral.

STEP BY STEP
Making the Joining Clasps

Make 2 identical clasps.

1 Cut a 12-inch (30.5 cm) length of each color of copper coated wire.

2 Twist the 4 wires together once.

3 Bend the combined wires in the middle, making a 6-inch (15.2 cm) length. Twist the wires together again at the cut ends, creating a loop at the folded end. Set the joining clasps aside.

Crocheting the Chain

4 Using the 4.00-mm yarn crochet hook and the 4 colors of coated copper wire held together, form a loop with the wire around your finger and make 1 chain stitch into the loop with the crochet hook.

5 Crochet a chain of 600 stitches.

6 Mark each 30th stitch by twisting a small piece of wire onto the stitch. This can be done as you crochet or after the chain is complete. Secure the markers loosely so they can be removed easily when the bracelet is finished.

Gathering the Chain

7 Insert the hook through the first stitch of the chain and through each 60th stitch. Put the loop of one joining clasp onto the hook, and pull it through all of the loops on the hook. Twist the joining clasp wire clockwise to keep it in place. This is one end of the bracelet.

8 Insert the hook through stitch number 30, counted from the first stitch, and then through each of the marked stitches that have not been used yet. Put the loop of the second joining clasp onto the hook, and pull it through all of the loops on the hook. Twist the joining clasp wire clockwise to keep it in place. This is the other end of the bracelet.

Finishing

9 On one end of the bracelet, put the loop on one of the joining clasps into the eye of one of the clasp parts.

10 Put the end of each of the joining clasp wires through the loop on the other end of the joining clasp, and pull the ends of the wires to tighten. Use the tapestry needle if you have problems threading the multiple wires through the loop.

11 To make the clasp stronger, put the joining clasp through the eye a second time, then fasten the clasp by twisting the joining clasp wire 3 times around one of the nearest stitches on the chain. Cut off the excess wire.

12 Repeat steps 10 to 12 on the other end of the bracelet.

13 Use flat-nose pliers to flatten and hide the cut wire ends. Remove the wire stitch markers.

VARIATIONS

• You can easily change the length of this bracelet by making the chain longer or shorter. For a shorter bracelet, chain 28 stitches between each marker. For a longer bracelet, chain 32 stitches between each marker.

• You can also make a necklace the same way, by beginning with a much longer chain.

PROJECT DIMENSIONS
3¹/₂ inches (8.9 cm) in diameter

MATERIALS
Coated copper wire, 4 colors of your choice, 28 gauge (0.33 mm), 1 spool (40 yards [36.6 m]) of each color

Sterling silver clasp

TOOLS
Wire cutters

Yarn crochet hook, 4.00 mm (size G U.S.)

Tapestry needle with large eye

Flat-nose pliers

cube pendant

EUGENIE KEEFER BELL

You will enjoy crocheting around a cube to fashion this intricate and appealing pendant. There is no pattern and no specific number of stitches, only an intuitive sense and an improvisational spirit.

STEP BY STEP

1 Mark the center of one side of the wooden or plastic cube and drill a hole large enough for the chain or cord to pass through easily. (Using a drill press will ensure the hole is centered on both sides of the cube.) If adding findings to the cord or chain, make sure the hole is large enough for the findings to pass through, or thread the pendant before attaching the findings.

2 Using the 3.50-mm steel crochet hook and the fine silver wire, make a loose chain of large stitches long enough to encircle the cube. Slip stitch to the first stitch to form a loop, and use the masking tape to lightly tape the chain to the cube. (The loose end will be covered by the crocheted mesh.)

3 Continue working on the same chain, and make large, loose stitches, now at a 90-degree angle to the first encircling loop, so that you go around another side of the cube. When crossing the first loop, slip stitch through it and continue the chain until it reaches all the way around the cube.

4 Change direction again, and continue to chain stitch around the cube, with large, loose stitches (they will tighten later). Slip stitch through some of the earlier stitches as you cross over them, gradually encasing the cube in the crocheted metal. Change direction often as you make this foundation covering of the cube. Keep the stitches loose now, so you can work back into them later. Continue until the entire surface of the cube is loosely covered.

5 Change to the 2.75-mm steel crochet hook, and use slip stitches to continue covering the cube in a random manner. Insert one or more chain stitches if it is difficult to reach the next place you want to cover. Try to keep the stitches loose, so you can continue to work back into them. As the crocheted structure becomes denser, change to the 1.50-mm steel crochet hook for finishing, and work tighter stitches.

6 When the cube is covered to your satisfaction, cut the wire, leaving a long enough tail to push the end back under the crocheted surface of the pendant. Pull the loose end of the wire through the last stitch and bury the end in the crocheted mesh.

7 Thread the pendant onto a chain or cord of your choice.

8 If using a ribbon or cord, tie the ends together for wearing, or add commercial findings. If using a metal chain, finish it with an S hook and loop. If the chain is long enough to go over the wearer's head, you can permanently close the chain by soldering or interlinking the two ends of the chain together (be sure to thread the pendant on first).

VARIATION

• For this project, 28 gauge (0.33 mm) coated copper wire also works well.

PROJECT DIMENSIONS
1¹⁄₄-inch (3.1 cm) cube

MATERIALS
Plastic or wooden cube, approximately 1¹⁄₈ inches (2.8 cm)*

Fine silver wire, 28 gauge (0.33 mm), 0.6 ounces (16 g)

Chain or cord of desired length

Findings of your choice (optional)

TOOLS
Drill or flexible shaft with bit to accommodate chain or cord

Drill press (optional)

Steel crochet hook, 3.50 mm (size 00 U.S.)

Masking tape

Steel crochet hook, 2.75 mm (size 1 U.S.)

Steel crochet hook, 1.50 mm (size 8 U.S.)

Wire cutters

Soldering kit, page 119 (optional)

* If using a wooden cube, select a hardwood. It will absorb less water or liquid silver cleaner when the pendant is cleaned.

fluffy silver necklace

INGER BLIX KVAMMEN

Made from a long strand of chain stitch gathered in loops to form a fluffy collar, this necklace provides ample practice using a crochet hook. The two-tone design is created by combining a background of dark, oxidized sterling silver wire with embellishments made of sparkling sterling silver.

STEP BY STEP

1 Using the sterling silver wire and the 4.00-mm yarn crochet hook, make a slipknot, leaving a 6-inch (15.2 cm) tail. Crochet a chain of 3,975 stitches. As you crochet, wind the chain into a ball or around a cardboard cylinder to prevent it from tangling. To make it easier to count your stitches, mark each 100th stitch by twisting a small piece of wire onto the stitch. Secure the markers loosely and remove them when you have completed the necklace.

2 Row 1: *Count 30 stitches back, and insert the hook into the 30th chain from the hook. Count 25 stitches more, and insert the hook into the 55th stitch. Count 20 stitches more, and insert the hook into the 75th stitch. There are now 4 loops on the hook. Yarn over hook, and pull a loop through all 4 loops on the hook. You have made 3 different-sized loops, using 75 chain stitches. Repeat from * 53 times. 3,975 stitches have been used and the necklace measures approximately 14 1/2 inches (36.8 cm), consisting of a sequence of loops in three different sizes.

3 Row 2: Crochet one row of slip stitches, making 1 slip stitch into each of the 53 stitches made in step 2 to strengthen the necklace.

4 Cut off the wire, leaving a 6-inch (15.2 cm) tail. Pull the tail through the last stitch to fasten off.

5 Use your hands to curl and lightly crush the chain loops toward the neckline to fluff the necklace.

Finishing

6 On each end of the necklace there is a 6-inch (15.2 cm) tail. Using the wire tails, fasten the clasp parts to the ends of the necklace.

7 Fasten the wire ends by twisting each of them 3 times around the last stitch, then cut the ends off with the wire cutters. Use the flat-nosed pliers to flatten the wire ends to make them less visible and less sharp.

8 Follow the manufacturer's instructions to prepare a warm solution of the liver of sulfur or liquid oxidizer. To oxidize the necklace, dip the entire piece into the warm solution briefly (30 to 60 seconds) and rinse immediately in cold water. If it is not dark enough, repeat the process.

(continued on page 40)

PROJECT DIMENSIONS
14 1/2 inches (36.8 cm) in diameter

MATERIALS
Sterling silver wire, 26 gauge (0.4 mm), approximately 4 1/2 ounces (138 grams)

Sterling silver clasp (hook and eye or magnet)

Liver of sulfur or liquid oxidizer

5 freshwater pearls

TOOLS
Yarn crochet hook, 4.00 mm (size G U.S.)

Wire cutters

Flat-nose pliers

fluffy silver necklace

Flower Embellishments

Make 5 identical flowers.

9 With the sterling silver wire and the 4.00-mm yarn crochet hook, make 6 chain stitches. Put the hook back into the first stitch, which will be the middle of the flower, and pull a stitch through.

10 Make 6 chain stitches. Put the hook through the middle again and pull a stitch through.

11 Repeat step 10 five more times to make a flower with 6 petals.

12 Cut the wire, leaving a 4-inch (10 cm) tail. Put one of the ends through a freshwater pearl and make the pearl stay in the middle of the flower. Put both wire ends on the back of the flower.

13 Fasten each flower onto the necklace where you want it to stay by twisting the wire ends on the flower around one of the chain loops on the necklace. Cut the wire ends off close to the chain.

VARIATIONS
• To make the necklace bigger, make a longer chain and repeat the loop-making procedure more times.
• The designer used two small sterling silver magnets for the clasp. A hook-and-eye clasp can also be used.

two layer pendant

ARLINE M. FISCH

two layer pendant

The front of this pendant is crocheted with fine silver wire, and the back is crocheted with purple-coated copper wire. The back is made slightly smaller than the front, so the purple does not show over the edge. As a final touch, pearls are sewn onto the center.

PROJECT DIMENSIONS
3 inches (7.6 cm) in diameter

MATERIALS
Round sterling silver wire, 14 gauge (1.62 mm), 12 inches (30.5 cm)

Sterling silver tubing with an inner diameter large enough for selected cord or chain

Fine silver wire, 28 gauge (0.33 mm), 1 ounce (31.1 g)

Coated copper wire, purple, 28 gauge (0.33 mm), 1 spool, 40 yards (36.6 m)

11 pearls, 3 mm (optional)

Sterling silver chain with S-hook clasp, 22 inches (55.9 cm) long

TOOLS
Wire cutters

Pipe or bracelet mandrel

Soldering kit, page 119

Mallet

Round file

Brass wire brush

Steel crochet hook, 2.75 mm (size 1 U.S.)

Steel crochet hook, 2.00 mm (size 4 U.S.)

Sewing needle

STEP BY STEP
Making the Wire Frame

1 Cut the 14-gauge round sterling silver wire to 9¼ inches (23.5 cm) to make a 3-inch-diameter (7.6 cm) circle. Form the wire into a circle using a pipe or bracelet mandrel. Solder the joint with hard solder, and then pickle to clean. Correct the shape of the circle with a mallet and a pipe or bracelet mandrel.

2 Using a round file, make 2 notches on the circle, well above center. Place the sterling silver tubing in the notches and solder it onto the frame using medium silver solder, then pickle to clean. Polish the wire frame with the brass wire brush (or tumble). Set the wire frame aside.

Crocheting the Pendant

3 Using the 2.75-mm steel crochet hook and fine silver wire, make a slipknot. Chain 3, and join with a slip stitch to form a ring.

4 Round 1: Chain 1, make 2 single crochets into each stitch, join with a slip stitch to the first chain stitch of the round (8 stitches).

5 Round 2: Change to 2.00-mm steel crochet hook. Chain 1, make 2 single crochets into each stitch, join with a slip stitch (16 stitches).

6 Round 3: Chain 1, make 1 single crochet into each stitch, join with a slip stitch.

7 Round 4: Chain 1, make 1 single crochet into each stitch, join with a slip stitch.

8 Round 5: Chain 1, *make 1 single crochet in next stitch, make 2 single crochets in next stitch. Repeat from * to end of round. Join with a slip stitch (24 stitches).

9 Round 6: Chain 1, make 1 single crochet into each stitch, join with a slip stitch.

10 Round 7: Chain 1, make 1 single crochet into the back loop of each stitch, join with a slip stitch.

11 Round 8: Chain 1, *make 1 single crochet into the back loop of the next stitch, make 2 single crochets into the back loop of the next stitch. Repeat from * to end of round, join with a slip stitch (36 stitches).

12 Rounds 9 and 10: Chain 1, make 1 single crochet into the back loop of each stitch, join with a slip stitch.

13 Round 11: Chain 1, *make 1 single crochet into each of the next 3 stitches, make 2 single crochets into the fourth stitch. Repeat from * to end of round, join with a slip stitch (45 stitches).

14 Round 12: Chain 1, make 1 single crochet into the back loop of each stitch, join with a slip stitch.

15 Round 13: Place the wire frame made in steps 1 and 2 against the back of the crocheted disc. Chain 1, make 1 single crochet into each stitch, going over the frame to attach it to the outside edge of the disc. Join with a slip stitch.

16 Cut the wire and draw the tail through the final loop. Pinch the disc gently to depress the center.

17 Using the purple-coated copper wire, follow steps 3 through 12 to make a second crochet disc for the back of the pendant. Cut the wire, leaving an 18-inch (45.7 cm) tail, and pull the tail through the last loop.

Finishing

18 Thread the tail of the copper coated wire onto a sewing needle. Stitch the purple disc to the back of the silver disc, sewing along the final row of silver stitches inside the frame to maintain the silver edge.

19 Thread the pearls onto a separate 6-inch (15.2 cm) length of fine silver wire and sew them to the silver side of the disc along the inside edge of the center depression made in step 16.

20 If desired, stitch the front and back discs together with a few stitches in the center of the discs. Bury the wire ends inside the pendant. Put the chain through the tube and fasten with the S hook.

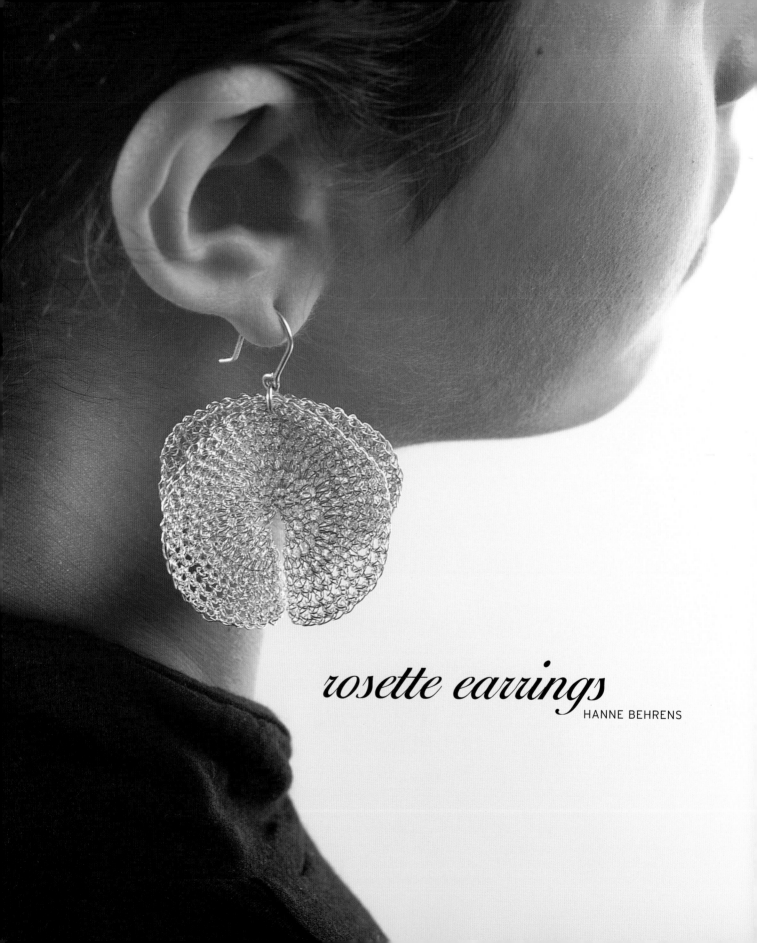

rosette earrings

HANNE BEHRENS

What better way to decorate your ears than with your own handiwork? These gorgeous earrings are crocheted in rounds, with the stitches forming small circles. After the crochet is complete, the circles are folded to form rosettes.

STEP BY STEP

1 Using the fine silver wire and the 1.30-mm steel crochet hook, make a slipknot. Chain 6 stitches and join with a slip stitch to form a ring.

2 Rounds 1 to 4: Chain 1 stitch, make 2 single crochets in each chain stitch, join with a slip stitch to the first stitch of the round.

Note: On the first round, capture the beginning end of the wire under the single crochet stitches because it is difficult to sew the end in later.

3 Rounds 5 to 7: Chain 1 stitch, make 1 single crochet in each stitch, join with a slip stitch to the first stitch of the round.

4 Cut the wire with wire cutters, leaving a 6-inch (15.2 cm) tail, and pull the tail through the last loop to fasten off.

Finishing

5 With the sewing needle, sew the ends of the wire carefully into the single crochet stitches.

6 Using the 20-gauge sterling silver wire, make two 1/8-inch (0.3 mm) jump rings and 2 ear wires.

7 Using the photo as a guide, bend each crochet circle in half with the round-nose pliers and bring the ends together to form a double layer.

8 Put a jump ring through both layers of crochet and place an ear wire in the ring in the center of each circle.

VARIATIONS

• To make the earrings with coated copper wire trim, you will need 1/4 ounce (8 g) of coated copper wire in the color of your choice. Work rounds 1 to 6 as described in steps 2 and 3. Cut the fine silver wire, leaving a 1 1/2-inch (3.8 cm) tail. On round 7, using the coated copper wire, chain 1, make 1 single crochet into the first stitch, then single crochet back into round 5 across the row, encasing row 6 in the coated copper wire. Join with a slip stitch to the first stitch of the round. Finish as described in steps 5 through 8, but place the jump rings in the folded ends of the circles.

• To make smaller rosettes, crochet fewer rows; to make larger rosettes, work more rows.

• To create a striped pattern, crochet alternating rows of fine silver and coated copper wire.

PROJECT DIMENSIONS
Each, 1 3/4 x 1 inch (4.4 x 2.5 cm)

MATERIALS
Fine silver wire, 30 gauge (0.25 mm), 1/4 ounce (8 g)
Sterling silver wire, 20 gauge (0.81 mm), for jump rings and ear wires

TOOLS
Steel crochet hook, 1.30 mm (size 10 U.S.)
Wire cutters
Sewing needle
Round-nose pliers

silver discs necklace

ARLINE M. FISCH

Encircle your neck with a piece made out of small discs crocheted with fine silver wire. The discs are joined with a continuous row of crochet made with lemon-colored coated copper wire.

STEP BY STEP
Crocheting the Discs

Make 11 identical discs.

1 Using the fine silver wire, make a slipknot 1½ inches (3.8 cm) from the end of the wire.

2 Round 1: Using the 2.75-mm steel crochet hook, make 18 single crochets into one of the sterling silver round wire rings. Join with a slip stitch to the first stitch of the round.

3 Round 2: Change to the 2.00-mm steel crochet hook. Chain 1, make 2 single crochets into each stitch, join with a slip stitch to the first chain stitch of the round.

4 Round 3: Chain 1, make 1 single crochet into each stitch, join with a slip stitch.

5 Cut the wire, leaving a 1½-inch (3.8 cm) tail, and draw the tail through the final loop to fasten off.

Finishing

6 To join the discs together, use the coated copper wire and the 2.75-mm steel crochet hook. Attach the coated copper wire by inserting the hook into the next stitch and drawing up a loop of coated copper wire. One loop is now on the hook. Yarn over hook, and pull the wire through the loop on the hook to secure.

7 Make one continuous row of single crochet as follows: Work across the top half of each disc, continue all the way around the last disc, then work across the bottom half of each disc, join with a slip stitch to the first stitch of the round.

8 Cut the wire, leaving a 1½-inch (3.8 cm) tail, and draw the tail through the final loop to fasten off.

9 Thread a separate length of fine silver wire onto a sewing needle and make a few stitches between each pair of discs above the center to shorten the length of the upper edge of the necklace and to give a final shape to the piece.

10 Work the ends of the wire into the last row of crochet on the necklace.

11 To attach a clasp, sew a single silver hook to the disc at one end of the necklace and an eye to the disc at the other end.

PROJECT DIMENSIONS
17 inches (43.2 cm) long, with 2-inch (5.1 cm) discs

MATERIALS
Fine silver wire, 28 gauge (0.33 mm), 3 ounces (93 g)

11 sterling silver round wire rings, 16 gauge (1.29 mm), ¾ inch (1.9 cm) in diameter

Coated copper wire, lemon, 28 gauge (0.33 mm), 1 spool, 40 yards (36.6 m)

Sterling silver hook-and-eye clasp

TOOLS
Steel crochet hook, 2.75 mm (size 1 U.S.)

Steel crochet hook, 2.00 mm (size 4 U.S.)

Wire cutters

Sewing needle

three-disc lariat

ARLINE M. FISCH

For this inventive necklace design, three discs are attached to three lengths of chain stitch. Each disc is crocheted in fine silver wire, then edged with coated copper wire for a bright, contrasting accent.

STEP BY STEP
Crocheting the Discs

Make 3 identical discs.

1 Using the fine silver wire, make a slipknot 1½ inches (3.8 cm) from the end of the wire.

2 Round 1: Using the 2.75-mm steel crochet hook, make 18 single crochets into one of the sterling silver round wire rings. Join with a slip stitch to the first stitch of the round.

3 Round 2: Change to the 2.00-mm steel crochet hook. Chain 1, make 2 single crochets into each stitch, join with a slip stitch to the first chain stitch of the round.

4 Round 3: Chain 1, make 1 single crochet into each stitch, join with a slip stitch. Cut the wire and draw the end through the last loop to fasten off.

5 Round 4: Attach the coated copper wire by inserting the hook into the next stitch and drawing up a loop of coated copper wire. One loop is now on the hook. Yarn over hook, and pull the wire through the loop on the hook to secure. Chain 1, make 1 single crochet into each stitch, then join with a slip stitch to the first stitch of the round.

6 Cut the wire and draw the tail through the final loop to fasten off. Work the end of the wire back into the row for several stitches.

Crocheting the Chains

7 With the 2.75-mm steel crochet hook and the fine silver wire and coated copper wires held together, make a slipknot, leaving a 4-inch (10.2 cm) tail. Make a 32-inch (81.3 cm) chain. Cut the wire, leaving a 4-inch (10.2 cm) tail, and pull the tail through the last loop of the chain to fasten off.

8 Repeat step 7 twice, making another 32-inch (81.3 cm) chain and a 26-inch (66 cm) chain.

(continued on page 50)

PROJECT DIMENSIONS
17 inches (43.2 cm) long, with 2-inch (5.1 cm) discs

MATERIALS
Fine silver wire, 28 gauge (0.33 mm), 1 ounce (31.1 g)

3 sterling silver round wire rings, 16 gauge (1.29 mm), ³⁄4 inch (1.9 cm) in diameter

Coated copper wire, color of your choice, 28 gauge (0.33 mm), 1 spool, 40 yards (36.6 m)

TOOLS
Steel crochet hook, 2.75 mm (size 1 U.S.)

Steel crochet hook, 2.00 mm (size 4 U.S.)

Wire cutters

Sewing needle

three-disc lariat

Finishing

9 Using a sewing needle and the wire tails at the ends of the chains, sew one end of each 32-inch (81.3 cm) chain to the edge of one crochet disc, placing them about ½ inch (1.3 cm) apart. Work the ends of the wire into the last row of crochet on the disc.

10 Repeat step 9, attaching the other end of each 32-inch (81.3 cm) chain to a second disc.

11 Using the wire tails at the ends of the chain, attach both ends of the 26-inch (66 cm) chain to the third disc, placing them about ½ inch (1.3 cm) apart.

12 Work the ends of the wire into the last row of crochet on the disc.

13 Thread the chains attached to the first and second discs through the center of the third disc. Open all chains to slip the necklace over your head.

VARIATION

• The crocheted discs can vary in size and color, and the number of chains can also be increased.

bead earrings

ANASTACIA PESCE

bead earrings

These crocheted bead earrings match the Five Stitch Chain on page 55. Made with increases and decreases and crocheted in spiral rounds, the tiny beads work up in almost no time at all.

PROJECT DIMENSIONS
Each, 5/8 inch (1.6 cm) in diameter

MATERIALS
Round fine silver wire, 28 gauge (0.33 mm), approximately 4.9 dwts

4 sterling silver discs, 1/4 inch (6 mm) in diameter

2 pieces of sterling silver tubing, each 5/8 inch (1.6 cm), 2 mm outside diameter (o.d.)

2 pieces of round sterling silver wire, each 3 1/2 inches (8.9 cm), 18 gauge (1.01 mm)

2 round sterling silver beads, 3 mm

TOOLS
Steel crochet hook, 1.00 mm (size 12 U.S.)
Scribe
Wire cutters
Dapping block and corresponding dap
Drill or flexible shaft with 18-gauge bit
Jeweler's saw frame and saw blades
File, #4 cut
Soldering kit, page 119
Finishing materials and tools of your choice
Polishing cloth or wheel
Chain-nose pliers
Chasing hammer
Steel block

STEP BY STEP
Crocheting the Beads

Make 2 identical beads.

Note: It may be necessary to make a few beads to achieve a matching pair. Pay careful attention to the number of stitches as you crochet. A difference of a stitch or two will change the proportions of each bead.

1 Using the 1.00-mm steel crochet hook and round fine silver wire, make a slipknot, leaving a 2-inch (5.1 cm) tail. Chain 3.

2 Join with a slip stitch to form a ring. Note: The shape is clumsy at this point, but make note of the stitch pattern. You can open the loops with a scribe to count the stitches and see the pattern more easily.

3 To create the top hemisphere of the bead, make 2 single crochets into each stitch until you have 12 stitches.

4 At this point, the shape of a shallow bowl is forming. To create the center of the sphere, make 1 single crochet into each stitch for 2 or 3 rounds.

5 Gently shape and refine the form, while the bowl is open and easier to manipulate.

6 To create the bottom hemisphere of the bead, *make 1 single crochet, skip 1 stitch. Repeat from * until the shape has closed up to a 1/8 inch (3 mm) hole and 3 stitches remain.

7 Use a scribe to ream, refine, and open the top and bottom holes on the sphere. Adjust the placement if the axis is not centered.

8 Cut the wire, leaving a 2-inch (5.1 cm) tail, and pull the tail through the last stitch to fasten off. Carefully weave about 1 1/2 inches (3.8 cm) of the tail into the bead, blending the weave with the stitch pattern. Cut off the excess wire.

Finishing

9 Prepare the finishing materials:

• Sterling silver discs: Dome in the dapping block to match the contour of the crocheted beads. Drill an 18-gauge hole in the center.
• Sterling silver tubing: Use the saw to cut the tubing to the desired length and file the cut ends.
• 18-gauge round wire: Use the saw to cut the wire to the desired length and file the cut ends.

10 Ball all ends of the cut wires to 1/16 inch (1.6 mm) with the soldering torch. Pickle and polish the wires.

11 For each earring, thread the disc and tubing onto the 18-gauge round wire. Slide the crocheted bead over the tube, then slide the second disc and a 3-mm bead over the ear wire.

12 Use chain-nose pliers to bend each ear wire at a 90-degree angle to make a hook 3/4 inch (1.9 cm) above the top of the bead.

13 Shape the back section of each ear wire into a gentle curve using the chain-nose pliers and your hands.

14 Tap the back side of the ear wires with the chasing hammer on a steel block to work harden. If necessary, snip the wires so they are both the same length.

15 Smooth the ends of the ear wires with the file to make them more comfortable to insert into the ear.

five stitch chain

ANASTACIA PESCE

Made of round fine silver wire and crocheted in a continuous spiral of single crochet, this luxurious and versatile necklace can be made in many different lengths and weights.

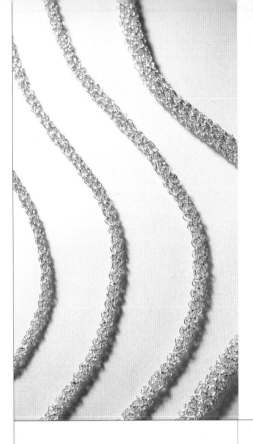

STEP BY STEP

Note: This chain is made as an upward-spiraling crocheted tube. Count the stitches often as you crochet. Dropping or adding a stitch will greatly disrupt the pattern of the chain.

1 With the 1.00-mm steel crochet hook and the round fine silver wire, make a slipknot, leaving a 2-inch (5.1 cm) tail. Chain 5.

2 Make 2 single crochets into the first chain to join into a ring.
Note: The shape is clumsy at this point, but make note of the stitch pattern. You can open the loops with a scribe to count the stitches and see the pattern more easily.

3 Round 1: Make 1 single crochet into each chain stitch. You now have 5 single crochet stitches.

4 Continue to make 1 single crochet into each stitch until you have the desired length.

5 Cut the wire, leaving a 2-inch (5.1 cm) tail, and pull the tail through the last loop. Gently pull to close the loop. Weave about 1 1/2 inches (3.8 cm) of the tail back into the chain, taking care to follow the pattern of the crochet stitches.

6 Tuck the ends of the wire into the chain. Roll the chain between your hands to refine the profile.

Finishing

7 Use the scribe to open a hole about 1/16 inch (1.6 mm) from each end of the chain.

8 Use the chain-nose pliers to open and thread one 14-gauge jump ring through each hole, and then close the jump rings.

9 Use the small jump ring to attach the hook to one of the 14-gauge jump rings. The other 14-gauge jump ring acts as the connector for the clasp.
Note: Do not pull the chain through a metal drawplate. This flattens the pattern of stitches and damages the tactile profile of the chain.

VARIATIONS

• This chain can be made to any length. It requires approximately 0.45 dwts of 28 gauge (0.33 mm) fine silver wire per inch (2.5 cm).

• Modify this chain by changing the wire gauge or stitch count.
Variation 1: 4 stitches, 28-gauge wire
Variation 2: 5 stitches, 28-gauge wire
Variation 3: 6 stitches, 28-gauge wire
Variation 4: 5 stitches, 30-gauge wire

PROJECT DIMENSIONS
24 inches (61 cm) long, 1/4 inch (6 mm) in diameter

MATERIALS
Round fine silver wire, 28 gauge (0.33 mm), approximately 11 dwts

2 jump rings, 14 gauge (1.62 mm), 4.5-mm outside diameter (o.d.)

Small jump ring to fit hook to ring on chain

Large heavyweight hook, approximately 10 mm

TOOLS
Steel crochet hook, 1.00 mm (size 12 U.S.)

Scribe or small awl

Wire cutters

Chain-nose pliers

pinwheel brooch

TINA FUNG HOLDER

Copper, silver, red, and blue wires are crocheted in stripes for each arm of this brooch. Each square is made separately using single crochet, and then the four pieces are stitched together to form a pinwheel.

STEP BY STEP
Crocheting the Squares

Make 4 identical pieces.

1 Using the 1.65-mm steel crochet hook and the copper-colored wire, make a slipknot, leaving a 3-inch (7.6 cm) tail. Chain 15 stitches.

2 Add the red wire. With the copper and red wires held together, *chain 1, turn, and make 1 single crochet into each stitch (15 stitches). Repeat from * until 8 rows have been completed.

3 Drop the red wire and add the silver wire. With the copper and silver wires held together, chain 1, turn, and make 1 single crochet into each stitch.

4 Drop the copper wire and add the blue wire. With the silver and blue wires held together, chain 1, turn, and make 1 single crochet into each stitch.

5 Drop the blue wire and add the copper wire. Cut the blue wire, leaving a 3-inch (7.6 cm) tail. With the silver and copper wires held together, chain 1, turn, and make 1 single crochet into each stitch.

6 Drop the silver wire and add the red wire. Cut the silver wire, leaving a 3-inch (7.6 cm) tail. With the copper and red wires held together, chain 1, turn, and make 1 single crochet into each stitch.

7 Cut the copper and red wires, leaving 3-inch (7.6 cm) tails. Pull the ends of both wires through the last stitch to fasten off.

Finishing

8 Fold each piece in half, and use the darning needle to stitch the two short ends together using the 3-inch (7.6 cm) tail from the beginning of the chain.

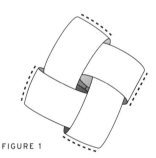

FIGURE 1

9 Using figure 1 as a guide, use a single strand of wire in the color of your choice to stitch the 4 squares into a pinwheel.

10 Bury all the wire ends inside the brooch by threading the wire onto the darning needle and sewing the wire to the interior of the structure.

11 Sew or glue the pin back in place.

PROJECT DIMENSIONS
1 3/4 inches (4.5 cm) square

MATERIALS
Coated copper wire, copper, 30 gauge (0.25 mm), 1 spool, 50 yards (45.7 m)

Coated copper wire, red, 30 gauge (0.25 mm), 1 spool, 50 yards (45.7 m)

Coated copper wire, silver, 30 gauge (0.25 mm), 1 spool, 50 yards (45.7 m)

Coated copper wire, blue, 30 gauge (0.25 mm), 1 spool, 50 yards (45.7 m)

Commercial pin back, 1 inch (2.5 cm) long

TOOLS
Steel crochet hook, 1.65 mm (size 7 U.S.)

Wire cutters

Darning needle

Hot glue gun and glue sticks or sewing needle and thread, to attach pin back

gourd pendant

ANASTACIA PESCE

Create a stylish and timeless pendant that is a pleasure to wear. Subtle variations in tension and stitch count will make each gourd a unique creation.

STEP BY STEP

1 Using the 1.00-mm steel crochet hook and 28-gauge fine silver wire, make a slipknot, leaving a 2-inch (5.1 cm) tail. Chain 3.

2 Make 2 single crochets into the first chain to join into a ring.

3 Make 2 single crochets into the next 2 stitches (6 stitches total). Note: The shape is clumsy at this point, but make note of the stitch pattern. You can open the loops with a scribe to count the stitches and see the pattern more easily.

4 Continue to make 2 single crochets into each stitch until you have 22 stitches.

5 Make 1 single crochet into each stitch until the side of the gourd is about ¼ inch (6 mm) high. The distinct form of a bowl should be taking shape. Gently refine the shape with your fingers, while the bowl is open and easier to manipulate.

6 To begin closing the form and to create the shoulder, *make 1 single crochet into each of the next 4 stitches, skip 1 stitch. Repeat from * until 11 stitches remain.

7 Make 1 single crochet into each stitch until the neck of the gourd is approximately ⅜ inch (1 cm) high.

8 Cut the wire, leaving a 2-inch (5.1 cm) tail, and pull the tail through the last loop to fasten off. Weave about 1½ inches (3.8 cm) of the tail back into the form, blending with the stitch pattern. Cut the excess wire.

(continued on page 60)

PROJECT DIMENSIONS
1½ inches (3.8 cm) long x ¾ inch (1.9 cm) in diameter

MATERIALS
Round fine silver wire, 28 gauge (0.33 mm), 3.5 dwts

Sterling silver jump ring, 16 gauge (1.29 mm) round wire, 7 mm in diameter

Round sterling silver wire, 12 gauge (2.05 mm), 1 inch (2.5 cm)

2 sterling silver attach rings, 20 gauge (0.81 mm), 3 mm, for bail

Bead or pearl, 6 mm (optional)

Sterling silver attach ring, 20 gauge (0.81 mm), 3 mm, for attaching the bead (optional)

Balled wire or head pin that fits through bead, ⅝ inch (1.6 cm) (optional)

Silver chain or satin or leather cord, length of your choice

Complimentary clasp, if chain is shorter than 30 inches (76.2 cm)

TOOLS
Steel crochet hook, 1.00 mm (size 12 U.S.)

Scribe

Wire cutters

Chain-nose pliers

Steel block

Chasing hammer

File

Drill or flexible shaft with 16-gauge bit

gourd pendant

Finishing

9 Using the scribe, open each loop at the top edge of the gourd shape. Open the jump ring and feed it through all of the opened loops. Close the jump ring with the chain-nose pliers. This reinforces the edge to which the bail will be attached.

10 To make the bail, place the 12-gauge round sterling silver wire on the steel block. Tap each end of the wire with the chasing hammer to flatten them into a paddle shape. Shape the flattened ends with the file. Use the drill or flexible shaft with the 16-gauge bit to drill a hole at the center of each paddle-shaped wire. Bend the paddle-shaped wire at the center to make a soft U shape.

11 Attach the bail to the gourd with the attach rings by inserting a ring into each hole in the paddle shapes and through the 16-gauge jump ring at the top of the crocheted form.

12 If desired, add a bead or pearl to the bottom of the gourd. At the center bottom of the gourd, use the scribe to open up loops to accept an attach ring. Open a jump ring and thread it through the attach ring. Close the jump ring. Thread the balled wire or head pin through the bead or pearl. Bend the wire at the top of the bead and cut it to ¼ inch (6 mm), then gently bend it into a loop. Use the chain-nose pliers to attach the bead or pearl to the ring at the bottom of the gourd. The extra jump ring allows for freer movement.

13 Hang the pendant on a silver chain or on a satin or leather cord with a complementary clasp. A 30-inch (76.2 cm) chain will fit over your head if you don't want to attach a clasp.

sphere necklace

ANNE MONDRO

sphere necklace

This necklace is made from 120 crocheted spheres that are sewn together to form a collar. The spheres are crocheted in the round using aqua coated copper wire, and some are embellished with gold accents.

PROJECT DIMENSIONS
20 inches long x 2 inches wide
(51 x 5 cm)

MATERIALS
Coated copper wire, aqua, 26 gauge (0.40 mm), 10 spools, 30 yards (27.4 m) per spool

Gold-plated sterling silver wire, 26 gauge (0.40 mm), 3 spools, 30 yards (27.4 m) per spool

Commercial gold-filled or gold-plated S-hook clasp with matching jump rings, large enough to suit the style of the necklace

TOOLS
Steel crochet hook, 3.50 mm (size 00 U.S.)

Wire snips

Round-nose pliers

Sewing needle

STEP BY STEP
Crocheting the Spheres

Make 120 identical spheres.

1 Using the 3.50-mm steel crochet hook and the coated copper wire, make a slipknot. Chain 6 stitches. Join with a slip stitch to form a ring.

2 Round 1: Make 1 single crochet into each stitch.

3 Round 2: Make 2 single crochets into each stitch.

4 Round 3: Make 1 single crochet into each stitch.

5 Round 4, decrease to narrow the sphere: *Draw a loop through each of the next 2 stitches. Yarn over hook, draw a loop through all three loops on the hook. 1 stitch decreased. Repeat from * to end of round.

6 Round 5: Make 1 single crochet into each stitch.

7 Using wire snips, cut the wire, leaving a 2-inch (5.1 cm) tail for sewing the form closed. Thread the tail through the last loop and pull tight. With your fingers, reshape the sphere and flatten the wire to create a uniform shape. Sew the wire through the top loops, pulling the wire tight as you stitch. This will close the top of the sphere. Wrap the end of the wire through a top loop several times to secure. Leave the remaining wire attached for sewing the spheres together.

Adding the Gold Trim

Add to 34 spheres.

Note: As you crochet the gold-plated wire onto each sphere, some flattening will occur. Try to avoid applying too much pressure to the form while crocheting.

8 Attach the gold-plated wire to a sphere by feeding the tail through a loop at the top of the sphere next to the wire left over from stitching the form closed. Twist the end of the gold-plated wire tightly with the round-nose pliers to fasten the wire to the sphere.

9 With the 3.50-mm steel crochet hook and the attached gold-plated wire, make 1 single crochet into an aqua-colored stitch. Continue to make 1 single crochet into each aqua loop to outline the circumference of the sphere.

10 Cut the gold-plated wire, leaving a 1-inch (2.5 cm) tail.

left attached after sewing the top of the spheres closed) together with the round-nose pliers. Using wire snips, cut the wires as close as possible. With pliers, curl the wires back on themselves.

12 Arrange the groups of 3 to form the necklace, making sure that the spheres overlap slightly. Assemble the necklace by stitching the groups together with 2-inch (5.1 cm) pieces of aqua-colored wire and a sewing needle. Where the spheres slightly overlap, feed the wire through both of them and twist the wire tightly with the round-nose pliers. Snip the wire ends as close as possible. Bend the wire back on itself with pliers. Continue to stitch the groups together until the desired length is achieved. Fill in any bare areas with leftover spheres. Keep stitching in the spheres until the necklace looks full and you are satisfied with its shape. Attach the jump rings and S-hook clasp to the ends of the necklace.

VARIATIONS

• Make a shorter necklace by using fewer spheres.

• Make a longer necklace that will slip over your head by using more spheres and sewing the ends together instead of attaching a clasp.

Feed the tail through the last gold loop and pull it tight. Feed the tail back through the same loop to secure the wire, and pull it tight again. Cut off the excess wire. Using the round-nose pliers, curl the end of the wire back on itself. Use your fingers to reshape the sphere.

Finishing

11 Arrange the spheres to create the desired shape for the necklace, placing the gold-trimmed spheres randomly. Group the spheres into sets of 3. Connect the 3 spheres by twisting the excess wires (the wires that were

calla pendant

ANNEGRET SCHMID

Crocheted leaves float gracefully on the end of a crocheted chain. The silver leaves are arranged around a tube made of soft, black iron wire. The pieces are crocheted separately and shaped with increases and decreases, then joined together to form a flower pendant.

STEP BY STEP
Crocheting the Iron Tube

1 Using the 1.50-mm steel crochet hook and 2 strands of iron wire held together, make a slipknot. Chain 10. Join with a slip stitch to form a ring.

2 Rounds 1 and 2: Make 1 single crochet into each stitch (10 stitches).

3 Round 3: Make 2 single crochets into stitches 1, 4, 7, and 10. Make 1 single crochet into all other stitches (14 stitches).

4 Rounds 4 and 5: Make 1 single crochet into each stitch.

5 Round 6: Make 2 single crochets into stitches 1, 5, 9, and 13. Make 1 single crochet into all other stitches (18 stitches).

6 Round 7: Make 1 single crochet into each stitch.

7 Round 8: Make 2 single crochets into stitches 2, 6, 10, 14, and 18. Make 1 single crochet into all other stitches (23 stitches).

8 Rounds 9 to 32: Make 1 single crochet into each stitch.

9 Cut the wire, leaving a 2-inch (5.1 cm) tail. Pull the tail of the wire through the last stitch to fasten off. Set the iron tube aside.

Crocheting the Large Silver Leaf

10 Using the 1.50-mm steel crochet hook and a single strand of the fine silver wire, make a slipknot. Chain 18 stitches.

11 Row 1: Skip 2 stitches, make 1 single crochet into the third stitch from the hook. Make 1 single crochet into each stitch across the row (16 stitches remain).

12 Rows 2 to 4: Make 1 single crochet into each stitch.

13 Row 5: Make 2 single crochets into stitches 2 and 15. Make 1 single crochet into all other stitches (18 stitches).

14 Row 6: Make 1 single crochet into each stitch.

15 Row 7: Make 2 single crochets into stitches 2 and 17. Make 1 single crochet into all other stitches (20 stitches).

16 Row 8: Make 1 single crochet into each stitch.

17 Row 9: Make 2 single crochets into stitches 2 and 19. Make 1 single crochet into all other stitches (22 stitches).

(continued on page 66)

PROJECT DIMENSIONS
1½ x 3¾ inches (3.8 x 9.5 cm)

MATERIALS
Soft black iron wire, 32 gauge (0.2 mm), 0.7 ounces (20 g)

Fine silver wire, 32 gauge (0.2 mm), 0.35 ounces (10 g)

Baby oil

TOOLS
Steel crochet hook, 1.50 mm (size 8 U.S.)

Wire cutters

Sewing needle

calla pendant

18 Row 10: Make 2 single crochets into stitches 2, 11, and 21. Make 1 single crochet into all other stitches (25 stitches).

19 Rows 11 to 14: Make 2 single crochets into the second stitch, the second to last stitch, and in each of the 2 center stitches. Make 1 single crochet into all other stitches. You have added 4 stitches in each row:
After row 11, you will have 29 stitches.
After row 12, you will have 33 stitches.
After row 13, you will have 37 stitches.
After row 14, you will have 41 stitches.

20 Rows 15 and 16: Make 2 single crochets into the second stitch, the second to last stitch, and in each of the 4 center stitches. Make 1 single crochet into all other stitches. You have added 6 stitches in each row:
After row 15, you will have 47 stitches.
After row 16, you will have 53 stitches.

21 Row 17: Make 1 single crochet into each stitch.

22 Row 18: Decrease as follows: Make 1 single crochet into the first stitch of the row, work the second and third stitches together. Make 1 single crochet into each stitch until you reach the center 2 stitches of the row. Work the center 2 stitches together. Make 1 single crochet into each stitch until you reach the last 3 stitches of the row. Work the next 2 stitches together. Make 1 single crochet into the last stitch. You have decreased 3 stitches (50 stitches remain).

23 Rows 19 to 29: Repeat row 18 in step 22. You have decreased 3 stitches per row on 11 rows, for a total of 33 decreases (17 stitches remain after row 29).

24 Rows 30 to 32: Decrease as follows: Make 1 single crochet into the first stitch of the row, work the second and third stitches together. Make 1 single crochet into each stitch until you reach the last 3 stitches of the row. Work the next 2 stitches together. Make 1 single crochet into the last stitch. You have decreased 2 stitches per row on 3 rows, for a total of 6 decreases (11 stitches remain after row 32).

25 Row 33: Make 1 single crochet into each stitch.

26 Rows 34 to 42: Skip 1 stitch, make 1 single crochet into the second stitch. Make 1 single crochet into each stitch to the end of the row. You have decreased 1 stitch per row on 9 rows, for a total of 9 decreases (2 stitches remain after row 42).

27 Row 43: Crochet the last 2 stitches together to make 1 single crochet. Cut the wire and pull the tail through the last loop to fasten off.

Crocheting the Small Silver Leaf

28 With a single strand of the fine silver wire and the 1.50-mm steel crochet hook, chain 12 stitches.

29 Rows 1 to 3: Beginning in the third stitch from the hook, make 1 single crochet into each stitch (10 stitches).

30 Rows 4 to 7: Make 2 single crochets into the second and second to last stitch of each row. Make 1 single crochet into all other stitches. You have added 2 stitches per row on 4 rows, for a total of 8 increases (18 stitches after row 7).

31 Rows 8 to 11: Make 1 single crochet into each stitch.

32 Rows 12 to 17: Make 1 single crochet into the first stitch of the row, work the second and third stitches together. Make 1 single crochet into each stitch until you reach the last 3 stitches of the row. Work the next 2 stitches together. Make 1 single crochet into the last stitch. You have decreased 2 stitches per row on 6 rows, for a total of 12 decreases (6 stitches remain after row 17).

33 Rows 18 to 21: Skip 1 stitch, make 1 single crochet into the second stitch and into each stitch to the end of the row. You have decreased 1 stitch per row on 4 rows, for a total of 4 decreases (2 stitches remain after row 21).

34 Row 22: Make 1 single crochet into each stitch.

35 Row 23: Crochet the last 2 stitches together to make 1 single crochet. Cut the wire and pull the tail through the last loop to fasten off. Using a sewing needle, work all of the wire ends back into the leaves. Sew the 2 silver leaves to the top of the iron tube using the silver wire.

Crocheting the Small Iron Leaves

Make 3 identical leaves.

36 With the 1.50-mm steel crochet hook and the iron wire, make a slip knot. Chain 4.

37 Row 1: Make 1 single crochet into each stitch (4 stitches).

38 Rows 2 to 4: Make 2 single crochets into the second and second to last stitch of each row. Make 1 single crochet into all other stitches. You have added 2 stitches per row on 3 rows, for a total of 6 increases (10 stitches after row 4).

39 Rows 5 and 6: Make 1 single crochet into each stitch.

40 Row 7: Make 1 single crochet into the first stitch of the row, work the second and third stitches together. Make 1 single crochet into each stitch until you reach the last 3 stitches of the row. Work the next 2 stitches together. Make 1 single crochet into the last stitch (8 stitches remain).

41 Row 8: Starting on the front right side of the iron tube, slip stitch the leaf to the top of the tube. Cut the wire and pull the tail through the last loop to fasten off.

42 Repeat steps 36 through 41 to make 2 more leaves, attaching them to the top of the tube in the same way and overlapping them slightly. Do not cut the wire after attaching the third leaf. The tube and these attached leaves form the flower.

Finishing

44 Using the attached iron wire,*make 14 single crochets around the top of the flower. Repeat from * to crochet 4 more rounds. End on the left side of the flower.

45 Continuing on the left, crochet a chain long enough to slip on over your head. Attach the chain to the right side of the flower with 2 single crochets. Use the same wire to make a second chain the same length, starting on the right side. As you crochet the second chain, connect it periodically to the first chain with a single crochet to keep them from tangling. Attach the end of the second chain to the left side of the flower with a single crochet. Cut the wire and pull the tail through the last loop to secure. Using a sewing needle, work the ends of the wire back into the structure. Rub the iron wire with baby oil periodically to prevent rust.

VARIATION

• Replace the iron wire with 28-gauge (0.33 mm) black-coated copper wire to eliminate the need to oil the black portion of the pendant.

silver & hematite beaded necklace

ARLINE M. FISCH

This simple necklace is made from nine lengths of chain stitch crocheted with fine silver wire, two of which are embellished with hematite beads. After the chains are crocheted, the ends are threaded into the rings of a sterling silver sliding catch.

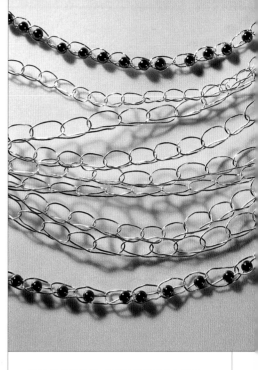

STEP BY STEP

Note: Start each chain with a slipknot, leaving a 6-inch (15.2 cm) tail. After each chain is complete, cut the wire, leaving a 6-inch (15.2 cm) tail, and pull the tail through the last loop to fasten off.

1 Thread 52 beads onto the 26-gauge fine silver wire. Using the 5.00-mm yarn crochet hook, crochet 9 chain stitches, then continue making chain stitches with a bead in each stitch until the chain is approximately 15 inches (38.1 cm) long. Make 9 chain stitches without beads. The chain should be approximately 16 inches (40.6 cm) long.

2 Using the wire and hook sizes listed below, crochet 7 chains of the following lengths without beads:
18 inches (45.7 cm), 3.50-mm hook, 26-gauge wire
19 inches (48.3 cm), 4.00-mm hook, 24-gauge wire
20 inches (50.8 cm), 5.00-mm hook, 24-gauge wire
21 inches (53.3 cm), 5.50-mm hook, 24-gauge wire
22 inches (55.9 cm), 6.00-mm hook, 24-gauge wire
23 inches (58.4 cm), 6.00-mm hook, 24-gauge wire
25 inches (63.5 cm), 6.00-mm hook, 24-gauge wire

3 Thread 82 beads onto the 24-gauge fine silver wire. Using the 3.50-mm yarn crochet hook, make a 24-inch (61 cm) chain with a bead in each stitch.

Finishing

4 Using the 6-inch (15.2 cm) tail at each end of the chains, thread the chains in order of size into the loops on the sliding catch.

5 Wrap each wire end through the loop several times, and then cut off the excess wire.

6 Use a soldering torch to bead the cut end of the fine silver wire, or bury the ends of the wire in the wrapped coils.

PROJECT DIMENSIONS
8 inches wide x 11 inches long (20.3 x 27.9 cm), with a 5-inch (12.7 cm) inner diameter

MATERIALS
134 hematite beads, 3 mm

Fine silver wire, 26 gauge (0.4 mm), 1¹/₂ ounces (46.7 g)

Fine silver wire, 24 gauge (0.51 mm), 1¹/₂ ounces (46.7 g)

Sterling silver sliding catch, 6 strand

TOOLS
Yarn crochet hooks in the following sizes:
3.50 mm (size E U.S)
4.00 mm (size G U.S)
5.00 mm (size H U.S)
5.50 mm (size I U.S)
6.00 mm (size J U.S)
Wire cutters
Soldering kit, page 119 (optional)

round spiral brooch

ARLINE M. FISCH

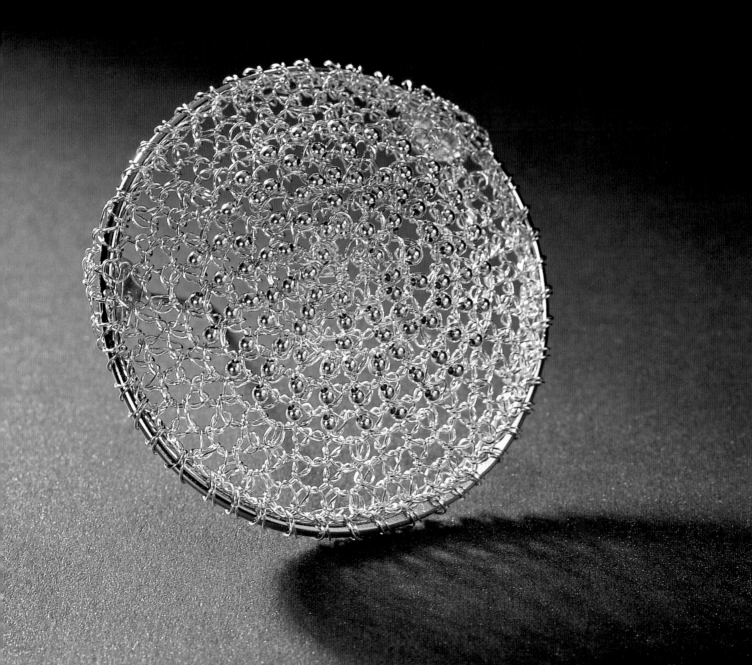

This sparkling circular brooch is a perfect introduction to crocheting with beads. Made in a spiral, you work single crochet stitches around and around in a simple pattern, sliding beads up to the crochet hook as instructed. The small silver beads can be replaced with pearls or glass beads for a different effect.

STEP BY STEP
Making the Wire Frame

1 Cut the 14-gauge round sterling silver wire to 9 1/4 inches (23.5 cm) to make a 3-inch-diameter (7.6 cm) circle. Form the wire into a circle using a pipe or bracelet mandrel. Solder the joint with hard solder, then pickle to clean. Correct the circle form using a mallet and a pipe or bracelet mandrel.

2 Solder the joint and catch to the sterling silver discs using medium solder, then pickle to clean. File a flat spot on the wire frame for the discs. Be sure to place them above the center.

3 Sweat solder the discs to the frame using extra-easy silver solder, then pickle to clean. Polish the wire frame with a brass wire brush and liquid soap (or tumble). Set the wire frame aside.

Crocheting the Brooch

4 Thread all of the small silver beads onto the fine silver wire. Wrap the end of the wire twice around the shank of the 2.00-mm crochet hook to form a double-stranded circle.

5 Round 1: Make 5 single crochet stitches into the center of the circle.

6 Round 2: Using the 1.90-mm crochet hook, make 2 single crochet stitches into each stitch, with beads (10 stitches).

7 Rounds 3 and 4: Make 1 single crochet into each stitch, with beads.

8 Round 5: Make 2 single crochets into each stitch, with beads (20 stitches).

9 Rounds 6 and 7: Make 1 single crochet into each stitch, with beads.

(continued on page 72)

PROJECT DIMENSIONS
2 1/4 inches (5.7 cm) in diameter

MATERIALS
Round sterling silver wire, 14 gauge (1.62 mm), 12 inches (30.5 cm)

Commercial sterling silver joint, catch, and pin stem

2 sterling silver discs, 22 gauge (0.63 mm), 1/4 inch (6 mm) in diameter

90 small silver beads, 2 mm

Fine silver wire, 28 gauge (0.33 mm), 1/2 ounce (15 g)

TOOLS
Wire cutters

Pipe or bracelet mandrel

Soldering kit, page 119

Mallet

File

Brass wire brush

Liquid soap

Steel crochet hook, 2.00 mm (size 4 U.S.)

Steel crochet hook, 1.90 mm (size 5 U.S.)

Sewing needle (optional)

round spiral brooch

10 Round 8: Add a second strand of the fine silver wire and work with 2 strands held together. *Make 1 single crochet into the next stitch, make 2 single crochets into the next stitch. Repeat from * to the end of the round (30 stitches).

11 Round 9: Make 1 single crochet into each stitch.

12 Round 10: *Make 1 single crochet into the next stitch, make 2 single crochets into the next stitch. Repeat from * around (45 stitches).

13 Round 11: Make 1 single crochet into each stitch.

14 Round 12: Place the wire frame against the back of the crocheted disc. Make 1 single crochet into each stitch, going over the frame to attach it to the outside edge of the disc.

15 Cut the wire, leaving a short tail, and draw the tail through the final loop.

16 Bead the cut ends with a soldering torch, or thread them onto a sewing needle and work them into the single crochet stitches.

VARIATIONS
• To make the structure flatter, add more stitches in rounds 6, 7, and 8.
• To make a more domed structure, make fewer increases in rounds 8 and 10.

crochet necklace

LILO SERMOL

crochet necklace

The spontaneous and dynamic form of this necklace makes it an exceptional piece. Made from 16 strands of chain stitch joined at the ends, and embellished with pearls, crystals, and obsidian snowflakes, it is elegant and easy enough for beginning crocheters.

PROJECT DIMENSIONS
7 x 9 x 1¹/₂ inches (17.8 x 22.9 x 3.8 cm)

MATERIALS
Tinned copper wire, 30 gauge
  (0.25 mm), 1 spool, 50 yards (45.7 m)

12 clear crystal chips

Silver-colored base metal wire,
  28 gauge (0.33 mm), 1 spool,
  40 yards (36.6 m)

8 freshwater pearls

Brass wire, 28 gauge (0.33 mm),
  1 spool, 40 yards (36.6 m)

7 snowflake obsidian chips

Non-tarnish silver wire, 28 gauge
  (0.33 mm), 1 spool, 40 yards (36.6 m)

Non-tarnish gold-colored wire,
  28 gauge (0.33 mm), 1 spool,
  40 yards (36.6 m)

Non-tarnish brass wire, 28 gauge
  (0.33 mm), 1 spool, 40 yards (36.6 m)

Coated copper wire, lemon, 34 gauge
  (0.15 mm), 1 spool, 125 yards (114.3 m)

Half-hard round sterling silver wire,
  20 gauge (0.81 mm), 12 inches (30.5 cm)

2 end caps

Closure hook or S-hook clasp

TOOLS
Steel crochet hook, 1.80 mm (size 6 U.S.)
Steel crochet hook, 3.25 mm (size 0 U.S.)
Small wire cutters

STEP BY STEP
Note: Start each chain with a slipknot, leaving a 6-inch (15.2 cm) tail. After each chain is complete, cut the wire, leaving a 6-inch (15.2 cm) tail, and pull the tail through the last loop to fasten off.

1 Using the tinned copper wire and the 1.80-mm steel crochet hook: Crochet a 17-inch (43.2 cm) chain. Crochet a 22-inch (55.9 cm) chain. String 5 clear crystal chips onto the wire, then crochet an 18-inch (45.7 cm) chain, spacing the crystals randomly along the chain.

2 Using the silver-colored base metal wire and the 1.80-mm steel crochet hook: Crochet a 21-inch (53.5 cm) chain. Crochet a 25-inch (63.5 cm) chain. String 5 freshwater pearls onto the wire, then crochet a 30-inch (76.2 cm) chain, spacing the pearls randomly along the chain.

3 Using the brass wire and the 1.80-mm steel crochet hook: Crochet an 18-inch (45.7 cm) chain. String 7 snowflake obsidian chips onto the wire, then crochet a 25-inch (63.5 cm) chain, spacing the chips evenly along the chain.

4 Using the non-tarnish silver wire and the 3.25-mm steel crochet hook: Crochet a 23-inch (58.4 cm) chain.

5 Using the non-tarnish gold-colored wire and the 3.25-mm steel crochet hook: Crochet a 20-inch (50.8 cm) chain. Crochet a 25-inch (63.5 cm) chain. String 7 clear crystal chips onto the wire, then crochet a 22-inch (55.9 cm) chain, spacing the crystals randomly along the chain.

6 Using the non-tarnish brass wire and the 3.25-mm steel crochet hook: Crochet a 24-inch (61 cm) chain. String 3 freshwater pearls onto the wire, then crochet a 21-inch (53.3 cm) chain, spacing the pearls randomly along the chain.

7 Using the lemon-colored wire and the 3.25-mm steel crochet hook: Crochet a 20-inch (50.8 cm) chain. Crochet a 25-inch (63.5 cm) chain.

Finishing

8 On each finished chain, pull one end to tighten the last loop. Repeat this step at the other end of the chain.

9 Cut a 6-inch (15.2 cm) length of 20-gauge half-hard wire and bend a loop 1 inch (2.5 cm) from one end of the wire.

10 Hang one end of all the crocheted chains on the loop by the last chain stitch. Wrap the short end of the 20-gauge wire around the group of chain stitches to join them together.

11 Take the other (straight) end of the 20-gauge wire and slip it through an end cap. Bend the wire at a 45-degree angle, make a loop, and slip in a closure hook or jump ring. Wrap the end of the wire around itself to secure the loop, and then cut off the end of the wire.

12 Repeat steps 9 through 11 on the other ends of the chains.

13 Add a separate closure hook to one end, or use an S hook.

VARIATION

• This is a very flexible piece that can be adjusted to be longer or shorter or to have a slightly different shape.

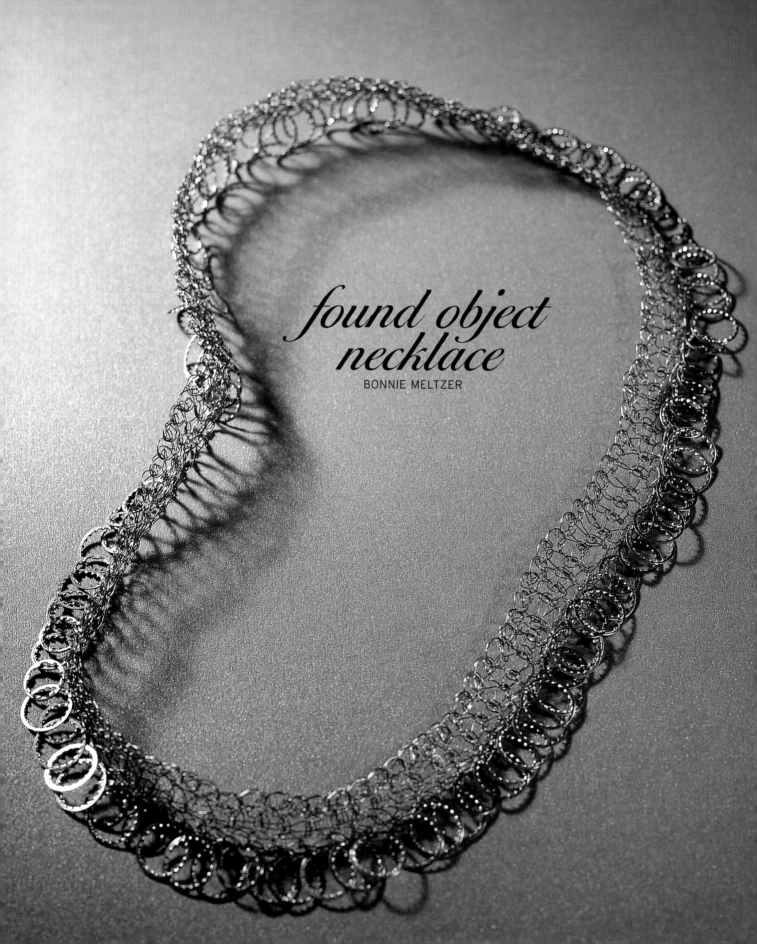

found object
necklace

BONNIE MELTZER

The combination of copper wire and metal washers makes a striking design. The technique used to attach washers to half double crochet is quite unusual. The necklace slips easily over the head and requires no clasp.

STEP BY STEP

1 Using the 4.00-mm yarn crochet hook and the coated copper wire, make a slipknot, leaving a 10-inch (25.4 cm) tail to sew the ends together later.

2 Chain 125 stitches.

3 Make 1 half double crochet into each stitch.

4 Turn the corner and make 1 half double crochet into the other side of each chain stitch, instead of flipping the crochet over as you normally do when working in rows. You will be working on the wrong side (back) of the necklace.

5 Work 1 row with washers as follows: *Yarn over hook, insert hook into next stitch, put a washer onto the hook, catch the wire with the hook, and pull the wire through the washer and all of the loops on the hook. Repeat from * to the end of the row. At the end of the row, go around the corner again as described in step 4.

6 Make 1 half double crochet into each stitch, inserting the hook through the back loop only.

7 Chain 2. Cut the wire, leaving a 6-inch (15.2 cm) tail, and pull the tail through the last loop to fasten off.

Finishing

8 Place the necklace on a table so it forms a ring. You may have to form the crochet gently with your fingers to get the final shape.

9 With a sewing needle, sew the ends of the necklace together, using the wire tails.

10 Cut the wire, leaving long enough tails to weave back through the structure. Make sure the wire end is on the right side (front) of the necklace, so it doesn't poke the skin.

11 Shape and flatten the necklace with your fingers. Slip it on, and pat it down to conform to your body. (If your necklace requires a lot of shaping, heat it with a hair dryer to aid the process.)

VARIATIONS

• You can use any kind of washers that you find pleasing. To select washers that are not too heavy, hold 125 of the washers you have selected in your hand to see how the weight feels.
• Choose washers in an assortment of sizes to add visual interest.
• If you don't want to slip the necklace over your head, attach a clasp instead of joining the two ends of the necklace together.

PROJECT DIMENSIONS
26 inches (66 cm) long

MATERIALS
Coated copper wire, color of your choice, 30 gauge (0.25 mm), 1 spool, 70 yards (64 m)

125 washers, rings, or any circular objects with a hole big enough to pass the crochet hook through

TOOLS
Yarn crochet hook, 4.00 mm (size G U.S.)

Wire cutters

Sewing needle

Hair dryer (optional)

amber & crystal bracelet

ZUZANA RUDAVSKA

Lovely gemstone beads of different shapes and colors make this bracelet incredibly attractive. Two pieces are crocheted separately, and then one piece is placed inside the other and they are sewn together at the edges.

STEP BY STEP

Crocheting the Gold-Filled Wire with Amber Beads

1 Thread the amber beads onto the gold-filled wire.

2 Using the 3.50-mm yarn crochet hook, make a slipknot.

3 Make 33 chain stitches with beads.

4 Join with a slip stitch to make a ring. This creates the first line of the bracelet.

5 *Chain 1. Work 1 single crochet into the back loop of each stitch, placing 1 bead into each single crochet. Repeat from * until 8 rounds of single crochet are completed and 297 beads have been used (including the beads on the foundation chain).

6 Cut the wire, leaving a 10-inch (25.4 cm) tail. Twist the end of the wire around the last loop 2 or 3 times to fasten off.

Crocheting the Sterling Silver Wire with Carnelian, Amethyst & Citrine Crystals

7 Mix the carnelian, amethyst, and citrine crystals together, and thread them onto the sterling silver wire.

8 Repeat steps 2 through 4, making 31 chain stitches to create the first line of the bracelet. Repeat steps 5 and 6 to make 9 rows with a total of 279 beads.

Finishing

9 Place the sterling silver beaded piece inside the gold beaded piece. The gold piece is visible from the outside and the sterling silver piece is only visible from the inside.

10 Align the two pieces so the ends of the 10-inch (25.4 cm) wire tails are on opposite sides of the bracelet. Use these wire ends and a sewing needle to sew the two pieces of the bracelet together at the edges.

11 Twist the ends of the wire around each other 3 times and cut off the excess wire. Bury the ends of the wire between the layers of the bracelet.

VARIATION

• To make a smaller or larger bracelet, adjust the number of stitches to fit around your wrist.

PROJECT DIMENSIONS
$3^{1}/_{2}$ x $3^{1}/_{2}$ x $2^{1}/_{4}$ inches (8.9 x 8.9 x 6 cm)

MATERIALS
297 amber beads (various shades), 6 or 7 mm

Gold-filled wire, 28 gauge (0.33 mm), 0.32 ounce (10 g)

279 carnelian, amethyst, and citrine crystals, 6 or 7 mm

Sterling silver wire, 28 gauge (0.33 mm), 0.32 ounce (10 g)

TOOLS
Yarn crochet hook, 3.50 mm (size E U.S.)

Wire cutters

Sewing needle

flourish scarf

KATHRYN HARRIS

This remarkable scarf, made from coated copper wire and beads, is crocheted with a single color of wire and nine colors of beads. Highlighted with an unusual beaded bullion stitch and trimmed with a scalloped crochet stitch, this is a challenging but very satisfying project.

STEP BY STEP
Before You Begin

Set aside 57 inches (144.8 cm) of beads of one color and 16 3/4 inches (42.5 cm) of a second color for the scalloped edge.

String the remaining beads onto the wire:
- Make sure the wire fits through all of the beads twice in order to finish ends of wire later.
- If you are using loose beads, use a bead spinner to load the beads onto the wire. Make the wire end into a hook.
- If the beads are in hanks (multiple strands strung on a thread), make sure the ends are knotted well before snipping one end of thread. Thread the beads directly onto the wire while the thread is still in place. Use a beading needle, if necessary.

In this project, when the instructions say "with beads," push a long section of beads up to the crochet hook so the wire is completely covered with beads. Make crochet stitches normally, using the bead-covered wire as if it were plain wire.

Give the wire some slack as you crochet. If the wire breaks as you are making a stitch, you are holding it too tightly. Even tension will come with practice. If necessary, insert the small crochet hook or straight pick into a stitch to open it up or adjust the shape.

Crocheting the Scarf

Refer to figure 1 on page 82 as needed for reference.

1 Using the 5.50-mm yarn crochet hook and the coated copper wire, make a slipknot. Chain 10 stitches with beads (width of scarf).

2 Row 1: Make 1 single crochet into each chain with beads (24 inches [61 cm] of beads), chain 1, turn.

3 Row 2: Make 1 single crochet into each stitch with beads (24 inches [61 cm] of beads), chain 1, turn.

4 Rows 3 to 5: Make 1 single crochet into each stitch (no beads), chain 1, turn.

(continued on page 82)

PROJECT DIMENSIONS
36 inches long x 5 inches wide (91.4 cm x 12.7 cm)

MATERIALS
Coated copper wire, color of your choice, 28 gauge (0.33 mm), 2.6 ounces (80 g) or 160 yards (146.3 m)

Seed beads, 9 colors of your choice, 9.6 ounces (298 g) total, any size that fits onto the wire

TOOLS
Yarn crochet hook, 5.50 mm (size I U.S.)

Bead spinner (optional)

Beading needle (optional)

Wire cutters

Small crochet hook or straight pick, to define stitches

FIGURE 1

flourish scarf

109, 110, 111 Beads - SC

106, 107, 108 Wire - SC

105 Beads - Bullions

102, 103, 104 Wire - SC

99, 100, 101 Beads - SC

96, 97, 98 Wire - SC

95 Beads - Bullions

92, 93, 94 Wire - SC

89, 90, 91 Beads - SC

86, 87, 88 Wire - SC

85 Beads - Bullions

82, 83, 84 Wire - SC

79, 80, 81 Beads - SC

76, 77, 78 Wire - SC

73, 74, 75 Beads - SC

70, 71, 72 Wire - SC

67, 68, 69 Beads - SC

64, 65, 66 Wire - SC

61, 62, 63 Beads - SC

58, 59, 60 Wire - SC

55, 56, 57 Beads - SC

52, 53, 54 Wire - SC

49, 50, 51 Beads - SC

46, 47, 48 Wire - SC

43, 44, 45 Beads - SC

40, 41, 42 Wire - SC

37, 38, 39 Beads - SC

34, 35, 36 Wire - SC

31, 32, 33 Beads - SC

28, 29, 30 Wire - SC

27 Beads - Bullions

24, 25, 26 Wire - SC

21, 22, 23 Beads - SC

18, 19, 20 Wire - SC

17 Beads - Bullions

14, 15, 16 Wire - SC

11, 12, 13 Beads - SC

8, 9, 10 Wire - SC

7 Beads - Bullions

4, 5, 6 Wire - SC

1, 2, 3 Beads - SC

START

5 Row 6: Work in bullion stitch as follows: chain 3 (no beads) *push 10 beads up to the crochet hook, yarn over hook 10 times, insert the hook into the next chain, pull up 1 loop, yarn over hook, pull the wire through all loops, chain 1 to complete. Repeat from * 8 times, chain 2, turn.

6 Rows 7 to 9: Repeat row 3 in step 4 (no beads).

7 Row 10: Make 1 single crochet into each stitch with beads, chain 1, turn.

8 Rows 11 and 12: Make 1 single crochet into the back loop of each stitch with beads, chain 1, turn.

9 Rows 13 to 15: Repeat row 3 in step 4 (no beads).

10 Row 16: Repeat row 6 in step 5 (bullion stitch with beads).

11 Rows 17 to 19: Repeat row 3 in step 4 (no beads).

12 Rows 20 to 22: Repeat rows 10 to 12 in steps 7 and 8 (with beads).

13 Rows 23 to 25: Repeat row 3 in step 4 (no beads).

14 Row 26: Repeat row 6 in step 5 (bullion stitch with beads).

15 Rows 27 to 29: Repeat row 3 in step 4 (no beads).

16 Rows 30 to 32: Repeat rows 3 (no beads), 4, and 5 (with beads) in step 4.

17 Rows 33 to 35: Repeat rows 11, 12, and 13 (no beads) in steps 8 and 9.

18 Row 36 to 83: Repeat rows 30 to 35 in steps 16 and 17 eight times.

19 Row 84: Repeat row 6 in step 5 (bullion stitch with beads).

20 Rows 85 to 87: Repeat row 3 in step 4 (no beads).

21 Rows 88 to 90: Repeat rows 3 (no beads), 4 and 5 (with beads) in step 4.

22 Rows 91 to 93: Repeat rows 10 to 12 in steps 7 and 8 (no beads).

23 Row 94: Repeat row 6 in step 5 (bullion stitch with beads).

24 Rows 95 to 97: Repeat row 3 in step 4 (no beads).

25 Rows 98 to 100: Repeat rows 3 (no beads), 4 and 5 (with beads) in step 4.

26 Rows 101 to 103: Repeat rows 3 to 5 in step 4 (no beads).

27 Row 104: Repeat row 6 in step 5 (bullion stitch with beads).

28 Rows 105 to 108: Repeat row 3 in step 4 (no beads).

29 Rows 109 to 111: Repeat rows 3 (no beads), 4, and 5 (with beads) in step 4.

Crocheting the Border Around the Scarf

30 Attach the coated copper wire to one corner on the front side of the scarf by making a loop of wire and pulling it through the first stitch on one corner of the scarf. Chain 1.

31 Round 1: Single crochet along the entire outer edge, making 1 single crochet into each stitch along the straight edges, and 3 single crochets into each corner stitch. Slip stitch into the first stitch of the round to join. Chain 1, do not turn.

32 Round 2: Make 1 slip stitch into each stitch around the entire edge of the scarf, adding 1 extra slip stitch into 2 stitches at each corner so the corners stay flat. Slip stitch into the first stitch of the round to join. Cut the wire, and pull the tail through the last loop to secure.

Crocheting the Scalloped Edge

33 Thread 57 inches (144.8 cm) of beads of one color, followed by 16 3/4 inches (42.5 cm) of a second color, onto the wire.

34 Row 1: With the right side (front) of the scarf facing you, make a loop of wire and pull it through the first stitch on the right edge of one short end of the scarf. Slip stitch into each stitch with beads.

35 Row 2: Chain 1 and turn, *chain 4, skip 1 stitch, make 1 single crochet into the next stitch. Repeat from * across bottom edge. Slip stitch into the last chain. Cut the wire, and pull the tail through the last loop to fasten off. Weave the wire tail back through the beads for 2 inches (5.1 cm) to hide the ends. Snip the wire closely.

36 Repeat steps 33 through 35 on the other short end of the scarf.

lilacs spiral necklace

This complex three-dimensional shape is actually easy to make. The spiral is fashioned from a long chain and only one row of double crochet, with five or six stitches worked into each chain stitch.

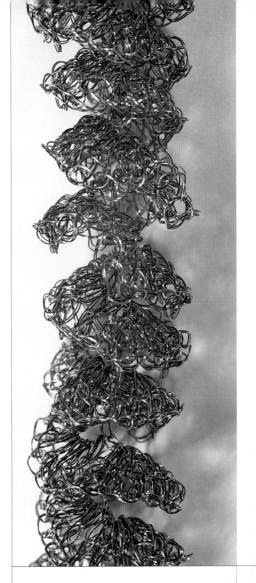

STEP BY STEP

Note: As you crochet, gently turn the piece counterclockwise to line up the spirals whenever the necklace gets twisted.

1 Using the 3.75-mm yarn crochet hook and both wires held together, make a slipknot. Chain 183 stitches.

2 Skip 3 chains, and in the fourth chain from the hook, make 5 double crochet stitches. In the next chain, make 6 double crochet stitches.

3 *Make 5 double crochets into the next stitch; make 6 double crochets into the next stitch. Repeat from * until 2 chains remain. Do not cut the wire.

Finishing

4 Chain 15 stitches. Bring the 15 chains around to the second empty chain to form a loop. Join with a slip stitch. This loop slips over the other end of the spiral to form a closure.

5 Cut the wire, and pull the tail through the last loop to fasten off.

6 Weave the wire tail back through the beads for 2 inches (5.1 cm) to hide the ends. Snip the ends of the wire closely.

VARIATION

• The necklace can also be closed with a hook-and-eye clasp sewn to the ends of the spiral.

PROJECT DIMENSIONS
25 inches long x 1 inch in diameter (63.5 x 2.5 cm)

MATERIALS
Coated copper wire, neon pink, 28 gauge (0.33 mm), 1/4-pound (114 g) spool, 500 feet (152.4 m)

Coated copper wire, purple, 30 gauge (0.25 mm), 1/4-pound (114 g) spool, 500 feet (152.4 m)

TOOLS
Yarn crochet hook, 3.75 mm (size F U.S.)

Wire cutters

eel trap necklace

HANNE BEHRENS

The undulating shape of this necklace is made by increasing and decreasing at regular intervals along a tube of single crochet. Finishing requires knowledge of bezel setting and solder construction to create a magnet clasp. The necklace can also be made long enough to sew the ends together and slip over the head.

STITCH PATTERNS USED

This project includes small and large circles that are crocheted at various intervals along the tube that forms the necklace. To keep the instructions from becoming too long, the steps for crocheting small and large circles are included here. Refer to these instructions whenever the Step by Step section mentions "small circle" or "large circle."

Crocheting a Small Circle

Round 1: Chain 2 stitches, *make 1 double crochet into each of the next 3 stitches, make 2 double crochets into the next stitch. Repeat from * 3 more times. Slip stitch to the beginning chain to join (21 stitches).

Round 2: Chain 2 stitches, *make 1 double crochet into each of the next 4 stitches, skip 1 stitch. Repeat from * 3 more times. Slip stitch to the beginning chain to join (17 stitches remain).

Crocheting a Large Circle

Round 1: Chain 2 stitches, *make 1 double crochet into each of the next 3 stitches, make 2 double crochets into the next stitch, repeat from * 3 more times. Slip stitch to the beginning chain to join (21 stitches).

Rounds 2 and 3: Chain 2 stitches, make 1 double crochet into each stitch. Slip stitch to the beginning chain to join.

Round 4: Chain 2 stitches, *make 1 double crochet into each of the next 4 stitches, skip 1 stitch, repeat from * 3 more times. Slip stitch to the beginning chain to join (17 stitches remain).

STEP BY STEP
Crocheting the Necklace

1 Using the 1.80-mm steel crochet hook and fine silver wire, make a slipknot, leaving a 6-inch (15.2 cm) tail for finishing the top of the tube by sewing into the first round of stitches. Chain 17 stitches, join with slip stitch to form a ring.

2 Rounds 1 to 7: Chain 1, make 1 single crochet into each stitch, slip stitch to the first chain stitch in the round to join.

(continued on page 88)

PROJECT DIMENSIONS
19 1/2 inches (49.5 cm) long

MATERIALS
Fine silver wire, 30 gauge (0.25 mm), 3 1/2 ounces (105 g)

Sterling silver sheet, 18 gauge (1.01 mm), 1/8 inch (3 mm) wide, 1 3/4 inches (4.4 cm) long

2 round magnets, 1/4 inch (6 mm) in diameter, 1/8 inch (3 mm) thick

Sterling silver sheet, 24 gauge (0.51 mm), 3/4 inch (1.9 cm) wide, 1 1/2 inches (3.8 cm) long, cut into 2 squares

Sterling silver tubing, 24 gauge (0.51 mm), 7-mm outer diameter (o.d.), 1 inch (2.5 cm) long, to fit inside the other tube

Sterling silver tubing, 24 gauge (0.51 mm), 1.4-cm outer diameter (o.d.), 1 inch (2.5 cm) long

TOOLS
Steel crochet hook, 1.80 mm (size 6 U.S.)

Sewing needle

Wooden dowel, 1/2-inch (1.3 cm) diameter

Pointed steel awl or pick

Soldering kit, page 119

Finishing materials and tools of your choice

Fast-drying adhesive

eel trap necklace

3 Beginning with round 8, crochet the tube in the following sequence:
Small circle
5 rounds single crochet
Small circle
4 rounds single crochet
Small circle
4 rounds single crochet
Large circle
3 rounds single crochet
Small circle
5 rounds single crochet
Large circle
4 rounds single crochet
Large circle
7 rounds single crochet
Small circle
3 rounds single crochet
Small circle
4 rounds single crochet
Large circle
3 rounds single crochet
Small circle
4 rounds single crochet
Small circle
4 rounds single crochet
Large circle

3 rounds single crochet
Large circle
4 rounds single crochet
Small circle
4 rounds single crochet
Small circle
3 rounds single crochet
Large circle
4 rounds single crochet
Small circle
3 rounds single crochet
Small circle
7 rounds single crochet
Large circle
4 rounds single crochet
Large circle
5 rounds single crochet
Small circle
3 rounds single crochet
Large circle
4 rounds single crochet
Small circle
4 rounds single crochet
Small circle
5 rounds single crochet
Small circle
7 rounds single crochet

4 Cut the wire, leaving a 6-inch (15.2 cm) tail, and pull the tail through the last loop to fasten off. Use a sewing needle to sew the tail into the last round of stitches.

5 Insert the dowel into the tube. Using the pointed awl or pick, place the dowel through the entire tube, passing it through the center of each circle. Slowly stretch each circle while keeping the single crochet areas in between pressed against the dowel to maintain the tubular form. Remove the dowel carefully when you are satisfied with the shape of the necklace.

Making the Tubular Magnetic Catch

6 Using the 1/8-inch (3 mm) 18-gauge sterling silver sheet, make 2 bezels to fit the magnets. Solder one bezel to the center of a 3/4-inch (1.9 cm) 24-gauge, sterling silver square (figure 1).

7 Cut the sterling silver tube into 1/2-inch (1.3 cm) lengths.

8 Solder one piece of tubing to the square with the bezel inside the center of the tube, as shown in figure 2. This makes half of the catch. Saw off the excess metal around the tube, file, and finish.

9 Solder the second bezel in the center of the second 3/4-inch (1.9 cm) 24-gauge, sterling silver square (figure 3).

10 Solder the square to the top of the smaller tube, with the bezel on the top of the tube, as shown in figure 4. Saw off the excess metal around the tube, file, and finish.

11 Make a second tube from the 7-mm, 24-gauge, sterling silver tubing to fit tightly inside the larger tube. One tube telescopes into the other, as shown in figure 5.

12 Put the magnets in the bezels temporarily and press them together. One tube will stand out from the other, with the magnets positioned on the inside (figure 6).

13 Use a 1/2-inch (1.3 cm) length of the 1.4-cm, 24-gauge, sterling silver tubing to press down over the smaller tube until the edges meet. Remove the magnets. Solder the tubes together. Pickle, clean, and polish or tumble the clasp to finish. Glue the magnets in place. Glue the sterling silver tubes neatly inside the ends of the crocheted tube.

VARIATIONS

• The crocheted tube could be made longer and the ends sewn together, to go over the head.

• The necklace does not need to be symmetrical. The large and small circles can be made in any order.

• To add color to the necklace, a row of single crochet in coated copper wire can be added to the edges of the circles after they have been stretched out. Be careful not to make the stitches too tight, or the circle will become smaller.

FIGURE 1

FIGURE 2

FIGURE 3

FIGURE 4

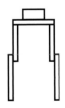

FIGURE 5

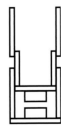

FIGURE 6

elizabethan partlet

JESSE MATHES

This partlet was inspired by the high collars worn by women in Elizabethan England. The collar consists of nine identical layers of modified Irish lace sewn onto a frame of single crochet. The pattern and construction couldn't be simpler, yet the results are spectacular.

STEP BY STEP

Note: This Irish crochet lace is made of alternating arches and ovals that get larger as the rows progress. The arches make up the structure of each layer; the ovals are decorative elements between the arches. An oval is always made into the same stitch where the previous arch stops.

Crocheting the Lace Layers

Make 9 identical pieces.

1 Using the 3.50-mm yarn crochet hook and the red and tangerine wires held together, make a slipknot. Chain 91 stitches.

2 Row 1: Skip 6 chains, and insert the hook into the seventh chain from the hook. Make 1 single crochet stitch. Make 3 chain stitches, and then insert the hook into the same seventh stitch of the foundation chain. Make 1 single crochet stitch. There should now be only 1 loop on the hook, and the 3 chain stitches should form an oval. Chain 5, skip the 3 chain stitches of the foundation chain closest to the oval, and

insert the hook into fourth chain. Make 1 single crochet stitch. There should now be only 1 loop on the hook, and the 5 chain stitches should form an arch. *Make another oval in the same chain stitch the arch ended in, and then make another arch. Repeat from * to the end of the foundation chain.

3 Row 2: When you reach the end of the foundation chain, make 7 chain stitches and insert hook into the third stitch of the last arch made (the top of the arch). This starts the second row. Make this row the same way as the first row, alternating between arches and ovals. The only difference is that the arches will span between the top of the arches of the first row, rather than from the foundation chain.

4 Row 3: Work as row 2 in step 3.

5 Row 4: Make 9 chain stitches and insert the hook into the third stitch (the top of the arch) of the last arch made. This starts the fourth row. Make this the same way as the previous rows, but make the ovals with 4 chain stitches and the arches with 7 chain stitches.

(continued on page 92)

PROJECT DIMENSIONS
12 x 12 x 2 inches
(30.5 x 30.5 x 5.1 cm)

MATERIALS
Coated copper wire, red, 28 gauge (0.33 mm), two $1/4$-pound (114 g) spools, 500 feet (152.4 m) per spool

Coated copper wire, tangerine, 28 gauge (0.33 mm), two $1/4$-pound (114 g) spools, 500 feet (152.4 m) per spool

Round copper wire, 14 gauge (1.62 mm), for clasp

TOOLS
Yarn crochet hook, 3.50 mm (size E U.S.)

Wire cutters

Sewing needle

Drill

elizabethan partlet

10 Cut the wire, leaving a 3-inch (7.6 cm) tail, and pull the tail through the last loop to fasten off.

Crocheting the Frame

11 Using 2 strands of the tangerine wire held together and the 3.50-mm yarn crochet hook, chain 12 stitches.

12 Row 1: Skip 1 chain. Make 1 single crochet into each chain stitch, chain 1, turn.

13 Row 2: Make 1 single crochet into each stitch, chain 1, turn.

14 Repeat row 2 until the frame is 13 1/2 inches (34.3 cm) long. Cut the wire and pull the tail through the last loop to fasten off.

Finishing

15 Sew the layers onto the frame using 1 strand of tangerine wire. Be sure to space them evenly on the base. If desired, sew 2 layers on at once to save time. Bury the ends of the wires in the crochet.

16 Using the 14-gauge copper wire, make a hook-and-loop clasp. Form a 2-inch (5.1 cm) loop and a 1 3/4-inch (4.4 cm) hook. Drill a few holes into each piece so they can be sewn securely onto the frame.

17 With a sewing needle and tangerine wire, sew the clasp onto the frame. Cut the wire about 3 inches (7.6 cm) from the last stitch and tie a knot around the closest stitch to secure. Wrap the end of the wire around that stitch a few times and cut the wire close to the wrap to hide the end.

6 Rows 5 and 6: Repeat row 4 in step 5 twice, noting that the top of the arch is now the fourth stitch rather than the third.

7 Row 7: Make 11 chain stitches, and insert the hook into the fourth stitch (the top of the arch) of the last arch made. Make this row the same as the others, but make the ovals with 4 chain stitches and the arches with 9 chain stitches.

8 Row 8: Repeat row 7 in step 7, noting that the top of the arch is now the fifth stitch rather than the fourth.

9 Row 9: Cut the red wire, leaving a 3-inch (7.6 cm) tail. Attach a second strand of tangerine wire. Repeat row 8 in step 8.

These airy bracelets are all made from hairpin lace crochet, an easy and fast technique using a crochet hook, multiple wires, and a stiff wire frame. By changing the dimensions of the frame and the color of the wire, bracelets can easily be made in different sizes and styles. Three variations are shown and included in the instructions.

bangle bracelets

ARLINE M. FISCH

bangle bracelets

For the Purple Lace Bracelet

PROJECT DIMENSIONS
3-inch diameter x 1 inch wide (7.6 x 2.5 cm)

MATERIALS
*Coated copper wire, violet, 28 gauge
  (0.33 mm), 1 spool, 40 yards (36.6 m)*
*Coated copper wire, lilac, 28 gauge
  (0.33 mm), 1 spool, 40 yards (36.6 m)*
*Coated copper wire, mauve, 28 gauge
  (0.33 mm), 1 spool, 40 yards (36.6 m)*

TOOLS
Hairpin lace frame, 1 inch (2.5 cm)
Steel crochet hook, 3.50 mm (size 00 U.S.)
Wire cutters
Sewing needle
Darning needle

STEP BY STEP

1 Using a strand of each color of wire held together, tie the wires to the 1-inch (2.5 cm) hairpin lace frame, leaving a 6-inch (15.2 cm) tail.

2 Using the 3.5-mm steel crochet hook, crochet a strip of 37 loops, 8½ inches (21.6 cm) long.

3 Cut the wire, leaving a 6-inch (15.2 cm) tail, and pull the tail through the last loop to fasten off. Remove the crocheted strip from hairpin lace frame.

Finishing

4 Using any color wire and a sewing needle, sew the beginning and end of the central crochet section together to form a circle.

5 Using the violet and lilac wires held together, make 1 round of single crochet, working into the large loops on the outside edge of the hairpin lace to finish the edge. Slip stitch to the first stitch to join.

6 Cut the wires, leaving 6-inch (15.2 cm) tails, and pull the tails through the last loop to secure. Thread the tails of the wires into a large darning needle and work the tails into the crochet structure, being sure to bury the ends.

7 Repeat steps 5 and 6 on the other edge of the bracelet.

For the Red Lace Bracelet

PROJECT DIMENSIONS
3½-inch diameter x 3½ inches wide (8.9 x 8.9 cm)

MATERIALS
*Coated copper wire, red, 28 gauge
  (0.33 mm), 1 spool, 40 yards (36.6 m)*
*Coated copper wire, gold, 28 gauge
  (0.33 mm), 1 spool, 40 yards (36.6 m)*
*Coated copper wire, pink, 28 gauge
  (0.33 mm), 1 spool, 40 yards (36.6 m)*
*Coated copper wire, brown, 28 gauge
  (0.33 mm), 1 spool, 40 yards (36.6 m)*

TOOLS
Hairpin lace frame, 3 inches (7.6 cm)
Yarn crochet hook, 5.00 mm (size H U.S.)
Wire cutters
Sewing needle
Darning needle

STEP BY STEP

1 Using a strand of each color of wire held together, tie the wires to the 3-inch (7.6 cm) hairpin lace frame, leaving a 6-inch (15.2 cm) tail.

2 Using the 5.00-mm yarn crochet hook, crochet a strip of 30 loops, 8½ inches (21.6 cm) long.

3 Cut the wires, leaving a 6-inch (15.2 cm) tail, and pull the tail through the last loop to fasten off. Remove the crocheted strip from the hairpin lace frame.

Finishing

4 Using any color wire and a sewing needle, sew the beginning and end of the central crochet section together to form a circle.

5 Round 1: Using the 5.00-mm yarn crochet hook and 2 strands of red wire and 1 strand of pink wire held together, make 1 round of slip stitch into the large loops on the outside edge of the hairpin lace to finish the edge. Slip stitch to the first stitch to join.

6 Round 2: Make 1 single crochet into each slip stitch. Slip stitch to the first stitch to join.

7 Cut the wires, leaving 6-inch (15.2 cm) tails, and pull the tails through the last loop to fasten off. Thread the tails of the wires into a large darning needle and work the tails into the crochet structure, being sure to bury the ends.

8 Repeat steps 5 through 7 on the other edge of the bracelet.

For the Two-Tier Lace Bracelet

PROJECT DIMENSIONS

3-inch diameter x 4 inches wide
(7.6 x 10.2 cm)

MATERIALS

Coated copper wire, purple, 28 gauge
(0.33 mm), 1/4-pound (114 g) spool,
500 feet (152.4 m)

Coated copper wire, violet, 28 gauge
(0.33 mm), 1/4-pound (114 g) spool,
500 feet (152.4 m)

Coated copper wire, gold, 28 gauge
(0.33 mm), 1/4-pound (114 g) spool,
500 feet (152.4 m)

Coated copper wire, tangerine, 28 gauge
(0.33 mm), 1 spool, 40 yards (36.6 m)

Coated copper wire, natural (clear),
28 gauge (0.33 mm), 1 spool,
40 yards (36.6 m)

TOOLS

Hairpin lace frame, 2 inches (5.1 cm)
Yarn crochet hook, 5.00 mm (size H U.S.)
Wire cutters
Sewing needle
Darning needle

STEP BY STEP

Make 2 identical strips.

1 Using the purple, violet, and gold wires held together, tie the wires to the 2-inch (5.1 cm) hairpin lace frame, leaving a 6-inch (15.2 cm) tail.

2 Using the 5.00-mm yarn crochet hook, crochet a strip of 30 loops, 8½ inches (21.6 cm) long.

3 Cut the wires, leaving a 6-inch (15.2 cm) tail, and pull the tail through the last loop to fasten off. Remove the crocheted strip from the hairpin lace frame.

Finishing

4 Using the 5.00-mm yarn crochet hook and the tangerine, gold, and natural wires held together, join the strips together lengthwise by making 1 row of slip stitch with each stitch catching 2 loops simultaneously (1 loop from the outside edge of each strip). This doubles the height of the bracelet.

5 Using a sewing needle and the tangerine, gold, and natural wires held together, sew the beginning and end of the central crochet sections together to form a circle.

6 Round 1: Using the purple, violet, and gold wires held together and the 5.00-mm yarn crochet hook, make 1 round of single crochet into the large loops on the outside edge of the hairpin lace to finish the edge. Slip stitch to the first loop to join.

7 Round 2: Using the tangerine, gold, and natural wires held together and the 5.00-mm yarn crochet hook, make a second round of single crochet by inserting hook into all original loops along with the first round of single crochet to create a firm edge.

8 Cut the wires, leaving 6-inch (15.2 cm) tails, and pull the tails through the last loop to fasten off. Thread the tails of the wires into a large darning needle and work the tails into the crochet structure, being sure to bury the ends.

9 Repeat steps 6 through 8 on the other edge of the bracelet.

hairpin lace choker

ARLINE M. FISCH

Made in a brown and silver two-tone design, this choker is a quick project. It is made from two strips of hairpin lace crochet that are joined together and fastened at the front with a button.

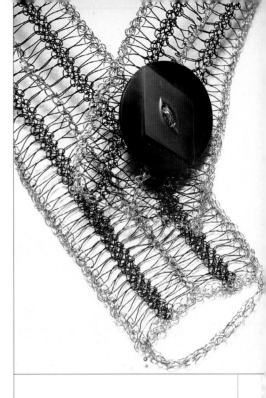

STEP BY STEP
Crocheting the Strips

Make 2 identical strips.

1 Tie the coated copper wire onto the hairpin lace frame, leaving a 6-inch (15.2 cm) tail.

2 Using the 1.65-mm steel crochet hook, make a strip 15 inches (38.1 cm) long, with 125 loops. Remove the crocheted strip from the hairpin lace frame.

Finishing

3 Using the fine silver wire and the 2.25-mm steel crochet hook, join the 2 long ends of the hairpin lace strips together as follows: *Make 1 slip stitch into 2 loops at once (1 loop from each strip). Repeat from * across the entire length of the strips. This makes one piece that is 2 strips wide.

4 Finish the outside edges of the collar with 1 row of slip stitch as follows: On the long edges, make 1 slip stitch into each loop of hairpin lace. On the short ends, make a series of slip stitches along the edge to continue the silver outline. There are no regular loops here, so make the slip stitches into the long sides of the last loops of each strip. Make enough stitches to maintain the size and shape of the end.

5 Starting at one corner, work 1 row of single crochet around the outside edge of the piece, making 1 stitch into every stitch across the edges and 3 stitches into each corner stitch. Be sure to insert the hook into both the brown loop and the silver slip stitch as you make each single crochet stitch. Slip stitch to join.

6 Cut the wire and pull the tail through the last loop to fasten off.

7 With the fine silver wire and the 2.25-mm steel crochet hook, make a double chain stitch (page 17) button loop, then use a sewing needle to sew the button loop onto one end of the choker.

8 Sew a large button onto the other end of the choker approximately 1 1/2 inches (3.8 cm) from the edge, so the ends overlap slightly when the choker is closed.

9 Weave in the ends of the wires and, if desired, bead the ends of the fine silver wire with a soldering torch.

PROJECT DIMENSIONS
14 1/2 inches long x 1 5/8 inches wide (36.8 x 4.1 cm)

MATERIALS
Coated copper wire, brown, 32 gauge (0.20 mm), 1 spool, 100 yards (91.4 m)

Fine silver wire, 30 gauge (0.25 mm), 1/4 ounce (7.8 g)

Large button for closure

TOOLS
Hairpin lace frame, 3/4 inch (1.9 cm)

Steel crochet hook, 1.65 mm (size 7 U.S.)

Steel crochet hook, 2.25 mm (size 2 U.S.)

Wire cutters

Soldering kit, page 119 (optional)

Sewing needle

hairpin lace necklace

ARLINE M. FISCH

The hairpin lace technique can be used to produce jewelry that is exceptionally majestic and alluring. The contrast of the copper and silver wire and the addition of seed beads to this necklace enhances its charm.

STEP BY STEP

1 Tie the coated copper wire to the $^3/_4$-inch (1.9 cm) hairpin lace frame, leaving a 6-inch (15.2 cm) tail. Using the 1.65-mm steel crochet hook, crochet a strip 19 inches (48.3 cm) long, with 130 loops. Cut the wire, leaving a 6-inch (15.2 cm) tail, and pull the tail through the last loop to fasten off. Remove the crocheted strip from the hairpin lace frame.

2 Tie the fine silver wire to the 1-inch (2.5 cm) hairpin lace frame, leaving a 6-inch (15.2 cm) tail. Using the 1.65-mm steel crochet hook, crochet a strip 19 inches (48.3 cm) long, with 130 loops. Cut the wire, leaving a 6-inch (15.2 cm) tail, and pull the tail through the last loop to fasten off. Remove the crocheted strip from the hairpin lace frame.

Finishing

3 Using the fine silver wire and the 1.65-mm steel crochet hook, join the strips length-wise as follows: *Make 1 single crochet into 2 loops at once (1 loop from each strip). Repeat from * across the entire length of the strips.

4 On the top edge, with the fine silver wire and the 2.25-mm steel crochet hook, make 1 single crochet into 2 loops at a time. This narrows and shapes the top edge of the necklace. Work a second row of single crochet, making 1 single crochet into each stitch from the first row.

5 On the bottom edge, thread 2 beads onto each hairpin-lace loop by squeezing each loop (gently) until it fits into the beads, placing the beads onto the loop, then reopening the loop with a blunt needle. This holds the beads in place and opens up the loops so it is easier to make the final crochet edge. Using the fine silver wire and the 2.25-mm steel crochet hook, make 2 rows of single crochet on the bottom edge of the necklace.

6 Cut the wire and pull the tail through the last loop to fasten off.

7 Sew a sliding-tube catch to each end of the necklace using a regular sewing needle with a double strand of the fine silver wire.

8 Weave in the ends of the wires and, if desired, bead the ends of the fine silver wire with a soldering torch.

PROJECT DIMENSIONS

7$^1/_2$-inch (19.1 cm) outside diameter, 4-inch (10.2 cm) inside diameter, 2 inches (5.1 cm) wide

MATERIALS

Coated copper wire, brown, 32 gauge (0.20 mm), 1 spool, 100 yards (91.4 m)

Fine silver wire, 30 gauge (0.25 mm), $^1/_2$ ounce (15.6 g)

260 seed beads, #8/0, color of your choice

Sterling silver sliding-tube clasp with 5 rings

TOOLS

Hairpin lace frame, $^3/_4$ inch (1.9 cm)

Steel crochet hook, 1.65 mm (size 7 U.S.)

Wire cutters

Hairpin lace frame, 1 inch (2.5 cm)

Steel crochet hook, 2.25 mm (size 2 U.S.)

Blunt needle

Sewing needle

Soldering kit, page 119 (optional)

hairpin lace collar

ARLINE M. FISCH

This Egyptian-style collar is made from three strips of hairpin lace crochet. The strips are joined together with a short silver strip at the neckline, a brown strip in the middle, and a long silver strip on the bottom of the collar. The collar closes at the back with hooks and eyes.

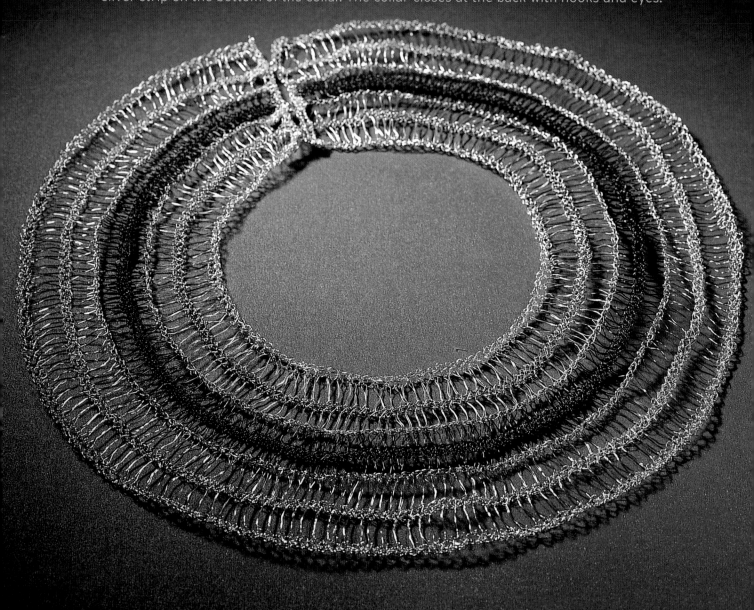

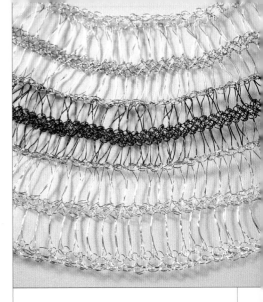

STEP BY STEP

1 Tie the coated copper wire to the ³/₄-inch (1.9 cm) hairpin lace frame, leaving a 6-inch (15.2 cm) tail. Using the 1.65-mm steel crochet hook, crochet a strip 22 inches (55.9 cm) long, with 150 loops. Cut the wire leaving a 6-inch (15.2 cm) tail, and pull the tail through the last loop to secure. Remove the crocheted strip from the hairpin lace frame.

2 Tie the fine silver wire to the 1-inch (2.5 cm) frame, leaving a 6-inch (15.2 cm) tail. Using the 1.65-mm hook, crochet a strip 22 inches (55.9 cm) long, with 150 loops. Cut the wire, leaving a 6-inch (15.2 cm) tail, and pull the tail through the last loop to secure. Remove the crocheted strip from hairpin lace frame.

3 Repeat step 2 to crochet a second strip in fine silver, 35 inches (88.9 cm) long, with 225 loops.

Finishing

Note: The strips are joined from bottom to top. The 35-inch (88.9 cm) silver strip is on the bottom of the collar, the 22-inch (55.9 cm) brown strip is in the center, and the 22-inch (55.9 cm) silver strip is on the top.

4 Using the fine silver wire and the 1.65-mm steel crochet hook, join the 22-inch (55.9 cm) brown strip to the 35-inch (88.9 cm) silver strip with a row of single crochet as follows: *Make 1 single crochet into 3 loops simultaneously (1 brown and 2 silver), make 1 single crochet into 2 loops simultaneously (1 brown and 1 silver). Repeat from * to the end of the row.

5 Using the fine silver wire and the 2.25-mm steel crochet hook, join the 22-inch (55.9 cm) silver strip to the top of the collar as follows: *Make 1 single crochet into 2 loops simultaneously (1 brown and 1 silver). Repeat from * to the end of the row.

6 Finish the top edge with a row of single crochet using the fine silver wire and the 2.25-mm steel crochet hook as follows: *Make 1 single crochet into 1 loop, then make 1 single crochet into 2 loops together. Repeat from * to the end of the row. Chain 1 and turn. Work a second row of single crochet, working 1 single crochet into each stitch.

7 Add edging to the bottom and sides of the collar using the fine silver wire and the 2.75-mm steel crochet hook. Starting at a top corner, work 1 row of single crochet, making 1 single crochet into each stitch and 3 single crochets into each corner stitch. Chain 1, turn, and work another row of single crochet making 3 single crochets into each corner stitch.

8 Cut the wire and pull the tail through the last loop to fasten off. Weave in the ends of the wires and, if desired, bead the ends of the fine silver wire with a soldering torch.

9 Sew 3 sets of sterling hook-and-eye clasps to the short ends of the collar at the top edge and at the joining of the strips.

PROJECT DIMENSIONS
5¹/₄-inch (13.3 cm) inner diameter, 3 inches (7.6 cm) wide

MATERIALS
Coated copper wire, brown, 32 gauge (0.20 mm), 1 spool, 100 yards (91.4 m)

Fine silver wire, 30 gauge (0.25 mm), 1¹/₂ ounces (46.7 g)

3 small sterling silver hook-and-eye clasps

TOOLS
Hairpin lace frame, ³/₄ inch (1.9 cm)

Steel crochet hook, 1.65 mm (size 7 U.S.)

Wire cutters

Hairpin lace frame, 1 inch (2.5 cm)

Steel crochet hook, 2.25 mm (size 2 U.S.)

Steel crochet hook, 2.75 mm (size 1 U.S.)

Soldering kit, page 119 (optional)

corn necklace

JOAN DULLA

Who could imagine that corn on the cob could shimmer with such sophistication? This necklace is made of 19 corncob-shaped gold beads interlaced with pearls. After crocheting the gold beads with the designer's unique crochet stitch, the beads and pearls are strung onto a silk cord.

STEP BY STEP

Note: It will take time and practice to make even loops and to establish a comfortable working rhythm. It is best to practice making several beads with coated copper wire before attempting to work in fine silver or 18-karat gold. The artist's crochet technique is explained in detail on page 28.

Crocheting the Corncob Beads

Make 19 identical beads.

1. Using the 18-karat gold wire, form a loop around the shank of the 1.65-mm steel crochet hook, and spin the hook twice to close the loop.

2. Repeat step 1 to make 3 more loops to form a four-leaf-clover shape.

3. Round 1: Insert the crochet hook through the front of one of the loops made in step 2. Catch the wire with the hook and pull a new loop through. Push the wire up onto the shank of the crochet hook to open up the loop and to create stitches of a uniform shape and size.

4. Remove the crochet hook completely and insert it into the next loop. Repeat step 3 to make another stitch. Continue making new stitches, working in a clockwise direction, to make a new round of 4 loops.

5. Round 2: Repeat steps 3 and 4 to make another round of stitches, but at the same time, add 1 new stitch after each existing stitch by inserting the crochet hook under the wire bridge between the loops of the previous row and pulling the wire through to create a new stitch (8 stitches).

6. Rounds 3 to 10: Continue making 1 stitch in each existing stitch and working in the round. As you crochet, form the top of the bead into a dome, then continue as a cylinder.

7. Round 11: *Combine 2 stitches together by inserting the hook into 2 adjoining stitches, then make 2 stitches normally. Repeat from * once (6 stitches remain in the round).

(continued on page 104)

(continued on page 104)

PROJECT DIMENSIONS
*24 inches (61 cm) long, with
3 inch (7.6 cm) gold beads*

MATERIALS
18-karat yellow gold wire, 28 gauge (0.33 mm), 1½ ounces (47 g)

18-karat yellow gold tubing, 12 inches (30.5 cm), 1.5 mm outer diameter (o.d.)

Silk cord, 24 inches (61 cm), for stringing

19 white pearls, 10 mm

18-karat gold clasp

TOOLS
Steel crochet hook, 1.65 mm (size 7 U.S.)

Wire cutters

Jeweler's saw and saw blades

corn necklace

8 Rounds 12 to 16: Make 1 stitch in each existing stitch.

9 Cut the wire, leaving a 4-inch (10.2 cm) tail, and pull the tail through the last stitch to fasten off.

10 Gather all the stitches together with the tail of the wire. Pull on the wire to close the end of the bead.

11 Work the tails into the crochet structure and clip off the excess wire.

Finishing

12 Roll the end of the bead in your fingers and pull gently until it looks like an ear of corn.

13 Measure the diameter at the top of the bead and use the jeweler's saw to cut the 18-karat gold tubing to fit inside. Cut 19 pieces of tubing, and place one piece inside each bead about one-third from the top. (The tubing hides the cord used for stringing the beads.) Tighten the stitches on each end of the tube so the tube doesn't slip out of the crocheted bead.

14 With the silk cord, string the crocheted beads alternating with 10-mm pearls, and knotting between each one. When stringing the crocheted beads, go through the tubing placed in the center of each bead.

15 Attach the clasp to the ends of the cord.

yellow gold
necklace

MICHAEL DAVID STURLIN

yellow gold necklace

PROJECT DIMENSIONS
*19¹/₂ inches (49.5 cm) long,
4.85 mm in diameter*

MATERIALS
*18-karat yellow gold round wire,
26 gauge (0.40 mm), 1 ounce
(30.85 g)*

*18-karat yellow gold sheet,
12 x 20 x 0.75 mm, and
6 x 15 x 0.75 mm for end caps*

*18-karat gold plumb gold solder,
hard, medium, and easy, 0.3 ounces
(9.8 g) each*

*18-karat yellow gold round wire for
jump rings, 1.5 mm in diameter,
45 mm long*

*18-karat yellow gold round wire for
toggle clasp, 2.5 mm in diameter,
90 mm long*

*18-karat yellow gold tubing,
26 gauge (0.40 mm), 1 inch
(2.5 cm), for toggle bar*

*18-karat yellow gold sheet for toggle
clasp tabs, 5 x 12 x 2 mm*

TOOLS
Wire cutters

*Knitting needle, 2.00 mm (size 0 U.S.),
or similar size awl*

Tapered spindle, 3.50 mm

*Round drawplate, size 8 mm to 5 mm,
31 holes*

*Round drawplate, size 5 mm to 2 mm,
31 holes*

Soldering kit, page 119

Non-marring mallet

Scribe

Assorted mandrels

Jeweler's saw and saw blades

File

Sandpaper

Dividers

Flexible shaft or twist drill

Drill bit, 1 mm

Pliers

The ancient and unusual technique used to make this stunning necklace is often called Viking knitting. It creates a tube of wire made of individual loops formed around a knitting needle. Although the stitch used to make this chain is easy, the finishing techniques require intermediate jewelry-making skills.

STEP BY STEP
Note: The artist's crochet technique is explained in detail on page 29.

1 From the 18-karat gold wire, cut one 28-inch (71.1 cm) length and thirty-five 20-inch (50.8 cm) lengths. Each 20-inch (50.8 cm) length of wire will produce approximately ¹/₂ inch (1.3 cm) of chain, depending upon the size and shape of the loops.

2 With the 28-inch (71.1 cm) piece of wire, make a coil of 7 long oval loops. Twist the coil of loops in the center and wrap the wire around the middle of the bundle. Spread out the loops to form a foundation resembling a flower with 7 petals. The loose end of the wire should pass outward through one of the loops.

3 To begin the chain and create each new loop, use your fingers to pass the wire over the top of itself, back into the loop from which it started, and exit outward through the next loop to the right.

4 Define the shape of each stitch by inserting the knitting needle into the stitch and moving the stitch up onto the shank of the needle. Draw the loop tight, and then remove the needle from the stitch. (To keep the size and shape of the loops even and symmetrical, it is important to maintain consistent tension when drawing the loops tight on the knitting needle.)

5 Repeat steps 3 and 4 for each new loop, working in a counter-clockwise direction, until 1 inch (2.5 cm) of wire remains.

6 When forming the last loop on a section of wire, leave the end of the wire inside the center of the chain. Add a new 20-inch-long (50.8 cm) section of wire by inserting the new wire into the next loop to the right of the last completed loop. Join the ends of the previous wire and the new wire by aligning and twisting them together to form a splice. Leave the splice inside the tube.

7 Continue forming loops and adding new sections of wire until the chain measures approximately 18 inches (45.7 cm). When forming the final loop of the chain, leave the end of the wire inside the center of the tube, as you did when adding new sections of wire.

Annealing, Straightening & Drawing the Chain

Note: Careful and thorough annealing is critical. If the chain is well annealed it will be easy to straighten out the spiral and draw the chain to a uniform shape. If the chain is not well annealed, it can make the finishing process rather difficult.

8 Coat the chain with a firescale-preventative solution of boric acid dissolved in denatured alcohol, and place the chain on a suitable surface for annealing. Light the soldering torch, ignite the alcohol solution, and allow it to burn off and coat the chain. As the alcohol flame subsides, begin to heat the chain evenly by moving the torch from one end to the other.

9 Keep the flame moving back and forth along the length of the chain and slowly bring it to a consistent, even temperature. Sustain the temperature for a brief interval of time, until the chain glows a soft red color in a semi-dark environment. (Do not heat the chain to a bright or cherry-red coloration.) Quench the chain in water. Pickle the chain, rinse it well, and dry it off.

10 Straighten the chain completely with your hands, then pull the chain carefully through a drawplate using no more than 3 holes. This will result in a smooth and uniform tube.

Making the End Caps

11 Using the 0.75-mm gold sheet (12 x 20 mm), fabricate a section of tubing 11 mm in length with an inner diameter of 4.8 mm for the end caps. Solder the seam of the tube closed using hard solder.

12 Scribe a center line in the middle of the tube and cut it in half to make 2 sections that are each 5 mm in length. Solder the tube sections to the remaining piece of 0.75-mm gold sheet (6 x 15 mm) using hard solder to close one end of the caps. Saw away the excess sheet and file the caps flush with the outer diameter of the tube.

13 Using the 1.5-mm round wire, fabricate a pair of jump rings with an inner diameter of 3 mm. Cut the jump rings apart and twist them closed, leaving the seam flush but unsoldered. File a flat surface onto each jump ring opposite the seam. Stand the jump rings upright with the flat spot on the top of the end caps and solder in place using medium solder.

14 Solder the end caps on each end of the crochet chain using easy solder.

Making the Toggle Clasp

15 Using the 2.5-mm round wire, form a circle for the opening of the toggle clasp with an outer diameter of 18 mm. Cut off the remaining length of wire and solder the circle closed using hard solder. Using a non-marring mallet adjust the roundness of the circle by tapping it on a ring mandrel until the shape is symmetrical.

16 Straighten the remaining section of 2.5-mm round wire and cut a length of 26-mm tubing for the toggle bar. Scribe a line at the center point of the toggle bar.

17 Set dividers at 6 mm and scribe a center line in the middle of the 2-mm piece of gold sheet for the toggle tabs. File a slightly rounded groove into each narrow end of the 2-mm gold sheet with a joint edge file or a round needle file.

18 Align the toggle bar and toggle circle with the corresponding grooves at either end of the tab sheet and solder in place using hard solder. Saw through the center line of the sheet to separate the 2 halves of the clasp. File the cut ends of the tabs flat and even with slightly rounded corners.

19 Using the dividers, mark a center point for a drill hole 2.5 mm from the end of the tab on each half of the clasp. Drill a hole to accommodate the jump ring beginning with a 1-mm twist drill. Using successively larger drill bits, enlarge the drill hole to 2.75 mm.

20 Gently twist open the jump rings on each end cap. Insert the toggle clasp components and twist the jump rings closed. Solder the jump rings closed with easy solder.

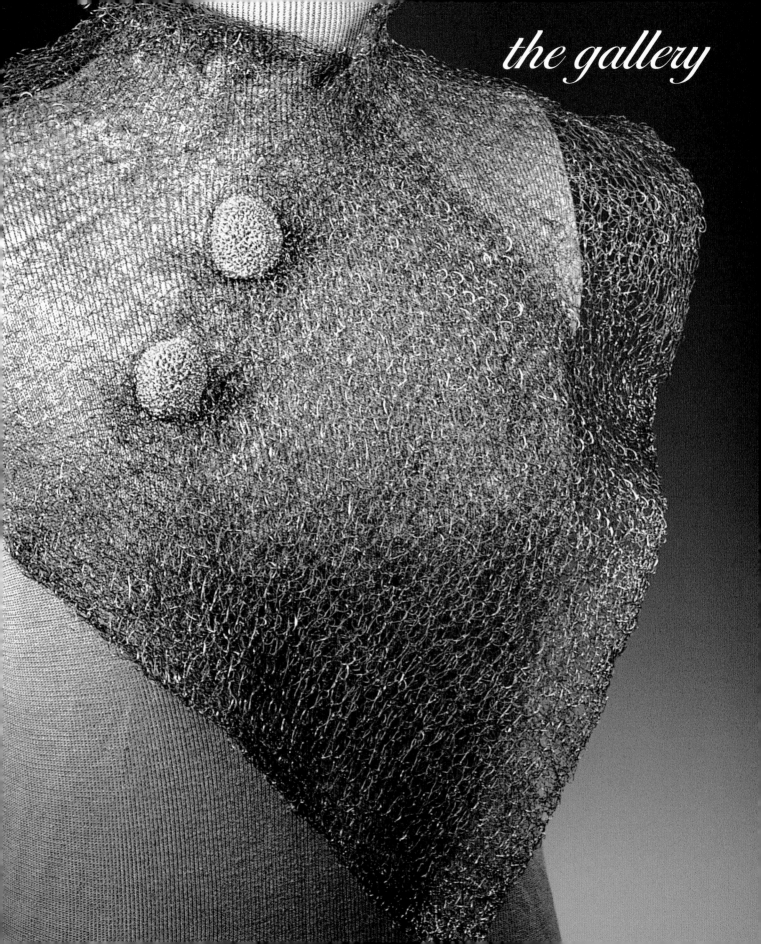

< INGER BLIX KVAMMEN
Untitled, 2001
Front length, 15 inches (38.1 cm)
Sterling silver wire,
18-karat gold wire; crocheted
Photo © Arline Fisch

^ ANASTACIA PESCE
Balancing Act, 2003
$^{15}/_{16}$ x 5$^5/_8$ x $^9/_{16}$ inch
(2.4 x 14.3 x 1.4 cm)
Fine silver wire, sterling silver,
18-karat gold; fabricated
Photo © artist

ˇ TINA FUNG HOLDER
Ezola I, 2000
21 x 1 inch (53.3 x 2.5 cm)
Copper wire, brass wire, silver wire;
crocheted over coil.
Photo © Jeff Bayne

^ MICHAEL DAVID STURLIN
Four Strand Crochet Necklace, 2002
17 x 8 x 1 inch (43.2 x 20.3 x 2.5 cm)
18-karat gold wire, diamonds;
crocheted, fabricated, set
Photo © Jon Balinkie, Camerawerks

ˇ EUGENIE KEEFER BELL
Untitled, 2003
1$^3/_4$ x 1$^3/_4$ x 1$^3/_4$ inches
(4.4 x 4.4 x 4.4 cm)
Stainless steel wire, Japanese ink;
crocheted
Photo © artist

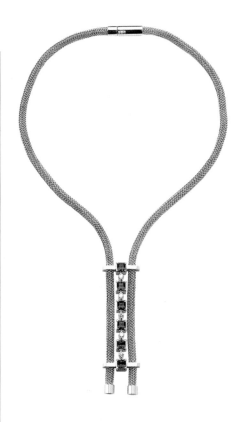

MICHAEL DAVID STURLIN
Red Tourmaline Waterfall Necklace, 2001
17 x 10 x 1 ½ inches (43.2 x 25.4 x 3.8 cm)
18-karat gold wire, tourmaline, diamond;
crocheted, fabricated
Photo © Jon Balinkie, Camerawerks

^ JOAN DULLA
Untitled, 2003
24 x 6 x 2 inches (61 x 15.2 x 5.1 cm)
Fine silver wire, sterling silver wire;
crocheted
Photo © W. Scott Mitchell

< ZUZANA RUDAVSKA
Red Celebration Bracelet, 2000
3 x 3 x 3 inches (7.6 x 7.6 x 7.6 cm)
Copper wire, freshwater pearls;
crocheted
Photo © P. Janek

> HANNE BEHRENS
Butterfly, 2004
Each, 2 x ¹³⁄₁₆ inch (5.1 x 2.1 cm)
Fine silver wire, 14-karat gold wire,
coral, lapis lazuli; crocheted
Photo © Ole Akhoj

< INGER BLIX KVAMMEN
Untitled Bracelet, 2002
Height, 4 inches (10.2 cm)
Pearls, buttons, fine silver wire,
coated copper wire; crocheted
Photo © Lene Stava Jensen

˅ JESSE MATHES
Elizabethan Gown, 2001-02
60 x 25 x 10 inches (152.4 x 63.5 x 25.4 cm)
Copper wire; crocheted
Photo © Kevin Montague

˅ LILO SERMOL
Autumn Flower, 2004
Front length, 27 1/2 x 31 1/2 inches (69.9 x 80 cm)
Copper wire, seed beads; tubular crochet
Photo © artist

> ARLINE M. FISCH
Greek Vases, 2003
Each, 4 inches (10.2 cm) tall
Fine silver wire, sterling silver
frames; crocheted
Photo © artist

˅ BONNIE MELTZER
Untitled, 2004
18 15/16 x 3 5/16 x 2 3/4 inches
(48.1 x 8.4 x 7 cm)
Copper magnet wire, beads, computer
parts, bifocal lens; crocheted
Photo © Patrick Smith

˄ KATHRYN HARRIS
Gaggle of Schmoozers, 2004
Each, 4 x 3 inches (10.2 x 7.6 cm)
Coated copper wire,
glass beads; crocheted
Photo © David Harris

> ZUZANA RUDAVSKA
Colorful Bracelet, 2003
3 x 3 x 3 inch (7.6 x 7.6 x 7.6 cm)
Copper wire, semiprecious
stones; crocheted
Photo © G. Erml

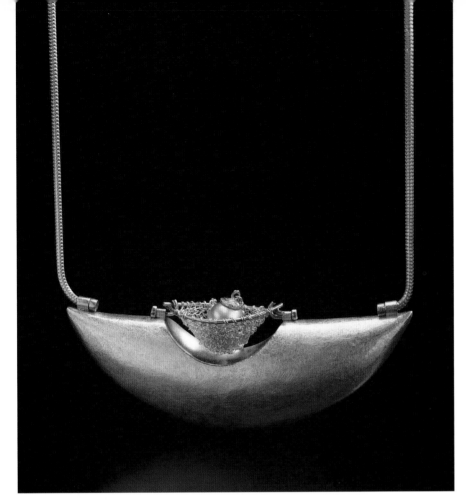

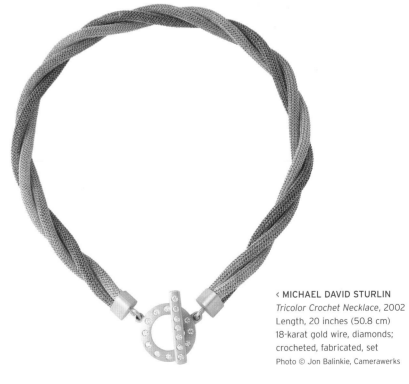

^ EUGENIE KEEFER BELL
Forms of Accumulation, 2000
2 x 2 x ⅛ inch (5.1 x 5.1 x 0.3 cm)
Fine silver wire, sterling silver frame,
sterling silver beads; crocheted
Photo © artist

⌄ TINA FUNG HOLDER
Untitled, 1985
7 x 6 x ½ inch (17.8 x 15.2 x 1.3 cm)
Copper wire, brass wire,
glass beads; crocheted over coil
Photo © Jeff Bayne

^ ANNE MONDRO
Untitled, 2004
18 x 2 x 2 inches (45.7 x 5.1 x 5.1 cm)
Coated copper wire, gold-filled metal
clasps; crocheted
Photo © artist

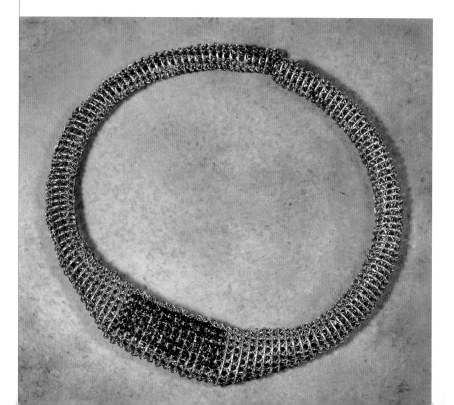

^ TINA FUNG HOLDER
Antherium, 2005
7 x 5 x ¾ inch (17.8 x 12.7 x 1.9 cm)
Coated copper wire, glass beads; crocheted
Photo © Jeff Bayne

^ ZUZANA RUDAVSKA
Turquoise Pendant, 2002
2½ x 2½ x ¼ inch (6.4 x 6.4 x 0.6 cm)
Turquoise, silver; fabricated
Photo © P. Janek

^ MICHAEL DAVID STURLIN
Crocheted Bracelets, 2003
Length, each 7¹⁵/₁₆ inches (20.1 cm)
18-karat gold wire, platinum;
crocheted, fabricated
Photo © Jon Balinkie, Camerawerks

v ZUZANA RUDAVSKA
White River Pendant, 2001
2¼ x 6½ inches (5.7 x 16.5 cm)
Gold-filled wire, sterling silver,
freshwater pearls; crocheted
Photo © G. Erml

v JESSE MATHES
Elizabethan Partlet #3, 2004
¾ x 11 x 11 inches (1.9 x 27.9 x 27.9 cm)
Silver-plated copper wire; crocheted
Photo © artist

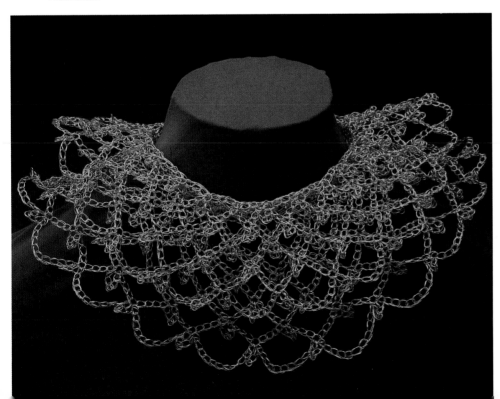

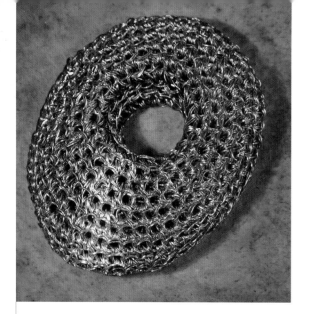

^ **TINA FUNG HOLDER**
Splash, 1985
3 x 2 x 1 inch (7.6 x 5.1 x 2.5 cm)
Copper wire, silver wire;
crocheted over coil
Photo © Jeff Bayne

^ **JESSE MATHES**
Elizabethan Partlet #5, 2004
1 x 12 x 12 inches (2.5 x 30.5 x 30.5 cm)
Silver-plated copper wire; crocheted
Photo © artist

ᵛ **LILO SERMOL**
Sawtooth, 2004
6¼ x ¹³⁄₁₆ inch (15.9 x 2.1 cm)
Brass wire, seed beads;
sawtooth stitch crochet
Photo © artist

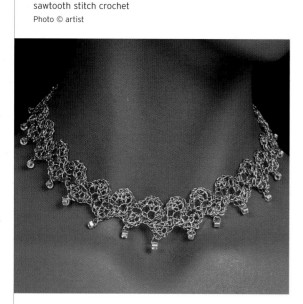

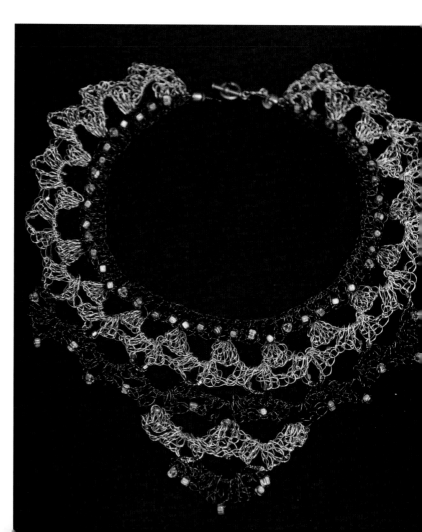

> **LILO SERMOL**
Untitled, 2003
8 x 10¼ inches (20.3 x 26 cm)
Copper wire, coated copper wire,
beads; scallop stitch crochet
Photo © artist

INGER BLIX KVAMMEN
Silver Nest with Pearls, 2004
Width from neckline, 6 ¾ inches (17.1 cm)
Sterling silver wire, freshwater pearls; crocheted
Photo © Lene Stava Jensen

^ **ANNE MONDRO**
Growth Bracelet, 2002
2 ½ x 6 inches (6.4 x 15.2 cm)
Coated copper wire, wool,
sterling silver clasp; crocheted
Photo © artist

ˇ **ZUZANA RUDAVSKA**
Copper Bracelet, 2002
4 x 3 x 3 inches (10.2 x 7.6 x 7.6 cm)
Gold-filled copper wire, carnelian,
amethyst, crystal, citrine; crocheted
Photo © P. Janek

‹ **HANNE BEHRENS**
Untitled, 2004
1 ¾ x ⁷⁄₁₆ x 8 ¾ inches (4.4 x 1.1 x 22.2 cm)
Fine silver wire, bead stringing wire,
lapis lazuli, sterling silver caps,
14-karat gold; crocheted, folded
Photo © Ole Akhoj

glossary

Annealing
The process of softening work-hardened metal by heating it with a torch to the appropriate temperature.

Awl
A small steel rod tapered to a sharp point, usually mounted in a wooden handle. Often used in leather work for making holes but can also be used for identifying and opening crochet loops before inserting a hook.

Bead Spinner
A small round bowl with a spin mechanism in the center used for threading large numbers of seed beads onto wire or thread. Available online or at bead shops.

Brass Wire Brush
Brushes made of 0.07-mm fine brass wire mounted in wooden or plastic handles. They are used with liquid dish detergent to produce a soft, satin finish on sheet metal.

Chain-Nose Pliers
Jeweler's pliers with semiround jaws with flat surfaces where they meet and tapering to a point from the pivot to the tip. Available in many sizes with both long and slender tips for working with wire.

Chasing Hammer
A small, slender hammer with one large, smooth face for striking punches and one round ball end, often mounted on a pistol-shaped handle.

Dapping Block and Punches
A steel or wooden block with various sizes of depressions that use conforming steel or wooden ball-shaped punches to dome flat discs of metal.

Disc Cutter
A block of steel with holes ranging from $1/8$ to 1 inch (3 mm to 2.5 cm) with cutting punches for stamping out discs in soft sheet metals up to 18 gauge (1.01 mm).

Dowels
Wooden rods in a range of diameters. Available from craft shops and lumber stores.

Drawplate
A thick steel plate with a series of conical-shaped holes used for reducing the diameter of wires and tubes.

Drill
An apparatus with an adjustable collet for holding a drill bit while cutting a hole. Drills can be hand or machine operated.

Drill Bits
Small steel rods with twisted cutting tips for use in all types of drills. Make sure that the bit is intended for drilling in metal.

Drill Press
A stand for holding a high-speed drill.

End Caps
Metal cones, half spheres, or fancy shapes for completing the ends of wire

or bead necklaces. Available from bead shops or jewelry-making suppliers.

Files
Jeweler's files come in a wide variety of shapes, sizes, and cuts. For small-scale work, needle files are the most useful, and a #4 cut will leave a fairly smooth surface.

Flat-Nose Pliers
Jeweler's pliers with two blunt and flat ends (no serrations). Available in many sizes from jewelry-making suppliers and some craft shops.

Flexible Shaft
A small, variable-speed motor with a hand piece mounted on a flexible arm and a foot pedal to control the speed. The hand piece holds a wide variety of cutting, grinding, and polishing bits.

Glue Gun
A small, pistol-shaped apparatus to hold glue sticks, which are heated and melt when the gun is plugged into an electrical outlet. Available from craft and home building shops.

Jeweler's Saw Frame
Jewelers use a U-shaped frame to hold a very fine saw blade that is designed specifically for cutting sheet metal. These are held vertically and moved in an up/down motion; they are available only from jewelry-making suppliers.

Joint, Catch, Pin Stem
Elements soldered to brooches for attachment to clothing.

Jump Ring
A round or oval ring used to join or link components. These may be formed individually using round-nose pliers or cut from a spiral of wire formed around a mandrel. They may also be purchased ready-made at bead and craft shops.

Liquid Oxidizer
Silver can be darkened to gray or black by dipping it into a solution of liver of sulfur dissolved in hot water, or by using a commercially available solution.

Pickle
A dilute acid solution used to clean oxides off a metal surface after heating. It is most effective when used warm, but it is highly corrosive and must be handled with extreme caution. It may be purchased in granular form to be dissolved in water.

Pin Back
A commercial finding that can be soldered, sewn, or glued to the back of a brooch.

Polishing
Crocheted wire should never be polished with a mechanical device, but it can be gently rubbed with a soft polishing cloth made especially for silver. Sheet metal parts can be finished with a polishing wheel or in a tumbler before being attached to wire constructions.

Round-Nose Pliers
Jeweler's pliers with two round jaws tapering from the pivot to the tip. Available in many sizes from jewelry-making suppliers and some craft shops.

Ruler
A small steel ruler or a cloth tape measure used to measure lengths and widths of material and completed elements.

Scribe
A sharply pointed steel rod used for marking sheet metal but may also be used in place of an awl for expanding crochet loops.

Soldering Kit
The tools and supplies used for soldering jewelry:
• Soldering torch
• Striker
• Heat-resistant soldering surfaces, such as charcoal blocks, firebricks, or ceramic plates
• Flux
• Flux brush or other applicator
• Hard, medium, and easy solder
• Snips for cutting wire solder
• Small embroidery scissors for cutting sheet solder
• Solder pick
• Tweezers
• Cross-locking tweezers with wooden handle
• Copper tongs
• Water for quenching
• Pickle

• Pickle warming pot, such as a slow cooker
• Safety glasses
• Fire extinguisher

Spindle
A tapered round steel implement, such as a machinist's center punch or a small bezel mandrel.

Steel Block
A small block of steel, highly polished on one surface, used when forming wire or sheet metal with a hammer.

Torch
There are many types of torches used by jewelers for annealing and soldering nonferrous metals such as silver, gold, copper, and brass. A small, handheld butane unit is sufficient for melting the end of silver wire to form a small ball.

Tube
Seamless tubes are commercially available in silver, copper, brass, and aluminum and are measured by their outside diameter (o.d.), their inside diameter (i.d.), and their wall thickness. They are cut to size using a jeweler's saw with a fine blade.

Wire Cutters
Small flush cutters or end cutters are used for clipping wires to specific lengths, or for cutting off excess wire.

contributing artists

HANNE BEHRENS is a traditionally trained Danish goldsmith who began experimenting with the use of textile techniques in the late 1970s while a special student at San Diego State University. She has many needleworking skills in her background—crochet and lace making in particular—which she was quick to translate into metal with great skill and precision. Initially, the Danish public didn't accept her jewelry using such techniques because it was considered too fragile, so Hanne sought ways to make it stronger and more durable. She explored braiding processes from the Viking era, making samples in metal using detailed diagrams from ethnographic books and journals, and continues to study both braids and baskets from many cultures. She also turned to lace making, a tradition from her birthplace in Tønder, Denmark, which she has successfully rendered in silver and gold wire to fashion graceful and elegant bracelets, brooches, and neckpieces.

Hanne accomplishes all her woven and braided work employing sterling silver and 18-karat gold, using materials in relatively heavy gauges constructed with the use of vises and pliers. Many of the structures are then soldered to fabricated borders, hinges, and clasps, and finished with the skills of the goldsmith. Until recently she had not used crochet, but was willing to return to it to explore some new ideas.

Hanne established her own studio at her home near Aalborg in the north of Denmark, showing and selling her work in exhibitions and galleries internationally. She has also organized and curated several major exhibitions, including one called *Braid*, which presented works in a variety of media, all utilizing the braiding process. She has won many awards in Denmark for her jewelry and is represented in a number of museum collections. Her most recent solo exhibition was presented by Mobilia Gallery in Cambridge, Massachusetts.

Her work has been described as requiring great skill to achieve a delicate balance in the relationship between form and appearance, as well as in the selection of materials and designs, resulting in classic and serene compositions. Each piece is inspired by both firmness and a feminine touch.

EUGENIE KEEFER BELL was born in San Diego, California. She earned both a bachelor and masters degrees in art from San Diego State University. Bell migrated to Australia in 1981, and earned a Ph.D. in architecture at the University of Western Australia. She has held university lecturing positions in gold- and silversmithing, art history, and architecture in Tasmania (1981–1986) and Western Australia (1986–2000). She now lives in Canberra, Australia's designed capital city, where she is senior lecturer in architecture at the University of Canberra. She writes widely on architecture, crafts, and design subjects, and maintains a studio practice in jewelry and metal.

Bell has held solo exhibitions in Australia, Japan, and the United States, and participated in more than 120 group exhibitions in Australia, the United States, South America, Europe, and Japan. Her work is represented in public collections, including the Smithsonian American Art Museum's Renwick Gallery, the National Gallery of Australia (Canberra), the National Gallery of Victoria (Melbourne), and the Art Gallery of Western Australia (Perth), and has been featured in numerous books and journals.

Works such as *Cube* are conceived as a kind of drawing, using a single line of fine silver wire, sometimes threaded with silver, gold, or glass spheres, interlaced into a dense structure and surface. These materially delicate pieces are supported on a base—a simple form cut or carved from wood or nylon—or worked over a constructed silver frame, which adds a degree of robustness, appropriate for their function as jewelry.

JOAN DULLA'S unique and striking style was shaped by her experiences, her passion to create, and her zest for the unconventional and unexpected. Using her own methods, Joan has taken a conventional crochet stitch and transformed it, allowing her to crochet metal to create sculpture and wearable art.

Just like her unique methods and eclectic style, each piece she creates is an original; no two pieces are identical. This gives each piece its own form and spirit. Nationally and internationally known for her crocheted gold, silver, and niobium jewelry and sculpture, Joan has had her work featured in *Lapidary Journal, Bead and Button*, and *Ornament* magazines. Joan has been nominated for the prestigious Niche Award in both gold and silver in the jewelry categories. She shows and sells her work at the Philadelphia Museum of Art Show, the Washington Craft Show, the One-of-a-Kind Show and Sale Chicago, and Craft Park Avenue in New York.

Joan says of her work, "When I crochet wire, I go into a meditative state, which soothes me. It feels like heaven. As the wire runs through my hands, I feel the coldness of the metal heat as I stretch and pull it. Its softness hardens as I manipulate it into place. It will do what I want. The air seems to float as I shape the bead, ball, or sculptural form. Noise disappears as I get lost in the process. Five hours later I have a necklace or a new sculptural form. The process fills my soul and makes my heart sing."

KATHRYN HARRIS learned to crochet as a child from her grandmother. She fell in love with the process, but was never particularly enamored of the results in yarn. As an adult, she began to crochet with wire and to combine the technique with beads. This revived her interest in crochet and she began to produce incredibly rich three-dimensional objects to wear.

Her graduate thesis, titled *Glitznglimmer,* consisted of a number of beaded necklaces, some crocheted, others made with wire and bugle beads, using a unique process that evolved out of her experiments with manipulating the materials.

Her extensive educational background ranges from an undergraduate degree in art history from the University of Michigan, to an MBA from New York University, to an MFA in jewelry and metalsmithing from San Diego State University. She worked in retailing in New York for a time, and at the Costume Institute at the Metropolitan Museum of Art, where she did restoration and exhibition display work. After moving to San Diego, she managed the library of the Fashion Institute of Design and Merchandising and organized the Costume Library for the San Diego State University School of Theatre, Television, and Film.

Kathryn is a self-proclaimed art and museum junkie who is particularly interested in architecture and the decorative arts, especially costume and the Japanese arts. She travels extensively to see art on site and to visit museum and private collections. She is an avid reader and researcher who finds endless fascination in discovering new ideas and ways of working, ranging from Victorian hair jewelry to Japanese kumihimo to her own unique bugle bead structures. At the moment, she is working more with vessel forms than

jewelry, using both crochet and the bugle bead process as a way to create forms that combine clarity, harmony, and beauty. Her work is shown regularly in galleries and invitational exhibitions around the United States, and it has been published in several books on beads and beadwork.

KANDY HAWLEY lived in New Zealand for several years. As a result, Maori art and architecture have had a great impact on her work, especially in her knowledge about various textile techniques. The Maori are innovative basket makers and often use these processes in their art, utensils, and even architecture. In addition, Kandy had a background in a number of needleworking techniques, including crochet, so it was natural for her to combine her experience with knitting and crochet with her studies in metal. As a graduate student at San Diego State University, she explored many aspects of metalwork but eventually settled on textile processes as the best way to construct large and airy sculptural forms, some of which became dramatic headdresses. She has successfully shown the hats, as well as freestanding objects related to primitive shelters, in a number of exhibitions and galleries. More recently she had the opportunity to produce machine-knitted wire jewelry as costume accessories for the film industry. Designing and producing the spiral crochet necklace project rekindled her interest in wire crochet.

TINA FUNG HOLDER has always focused on alternative uses for both techniques and materials, stretching traditional boundaries and developing her own unique approach. She combines traditional techniques with alternative materials, and introduces traditional materials outside of their expected usage. Her signature for many years has been the safety pin, which she transforms into elegant and refined jewelry using an understructure of single crochet in perle cotton. She has also explored crochet in wire using multiple strands to create dense structures that are powerful in form and rich in color.

Tina has lived in the United States since 1969. She received both a BFA and an MFA from the School of the Art Institute of Chicago, but her informal training was acquired from growing up in a rural village in Guyana, South America, and from her research at The Field Museum in Chicago. In 1996 she moved from Chicago to the rural Northwoods area of Wisconsin, where she maintains an active studio practice in both jewelry and basket making, regularly showing her work in museum and gallery exhibitions around the country. Her work is represented in a number of public collections, including the Museum of Arts and Design (formerly the American Craft Museum) and the Smithsonian American Art Museum's Renwick Gallery.

INGER BLIX KVAMMEN lives in Kirkenes, in the northeastern tip of Norway. Her background in the traditional weaving, knitting, and other textile arts of her native land has led her to consider those techniques for working in metal. Trained in art education and art history, she initially used bits of fabric to fashion necklaces but soon turned to wire in silver, copper, and gold as more suitable for jewelry.

Although she has explored a number of processes, the majority of her work is either woven on a fixed heddle loom or crocheted using simple stitches. She doesn't have a goldsmithing background, but she describes this limitation as influencing her to find new solutions in the techniques she does know. Some of these include the use of buttons and simple hooks and eyes as fastenings, although she has studied basic metalworking in order to construct clasps and finials for particular pieces.

Inger's work has been shown in solo and group exhibitions in Norway, Russia, England, and the United States, and she is represented by a number of galleries, including Velvet da Vinci in San Francisco; Julie Artisans in New York City; Mobilia in Cambridge, Massachusetts; and Electrum Gallery in London.

JESSE MATHES began studying art in 1998 at San Diego State University. An early interest in beaded jewelry led to a focus on jewelry and metalwork courses, where she was encouraged to create work outside the realms of traditional body adornment, and to unite craft with fine art. During a semester studying at the University of Dundee in Scotland, Jesse became interested in the clothing of Queen Elizabeth I. Upon returning from this experience, she enrolled in a course in textile techniques in metal with Arline M. Fisch, and began creating crocheted garments inspired by Elizabethan clothing, which she researched extensively. Enrolled in the graduate program in jewelry and metalsmithing at Indiana University, she was encouraged to continue exploring unconventional body adornment in a variety of metals and techniques. She completed an MFA degree in 2004, and operated Gallery Mathes, which featured contemporary jewelry and fine craft in Terra Haute, Indiana. She now lives in Chicago.

BONNIE MELTZER was born with a crochet hook in one hand and a purple crayon in the other. Thus began her use of mixing materials together. In the 1970s, she began to crochet electronics wire. At the same surplus store where she discovered magnet wire—a beautiful, colorful, and very flexible wire—she found other computer widgets and thingamabobs. Their intrinsic beauty made its way into her work. Since that time, she has also learned to master real working computers, which she uses to design large-scale artworks and to produce images that are part of the sculptures. In work that has so many disparate elements—crochet, found objects, and digital photography—crochet links everything visually, and sometimes even structurally.

Bonnie began making jewelry as a kind of sketchbook, working out ideas and testing out materials for larger pieces. She found it wonderful to complete work in just hours rather than days, weeks, or months. The jewelry has now evolved into a whole distinct category of its own. All of the designs are one-of-a-kind, a necessity when using found objects, but more fun to make as well. Bonnie also wanted to wear her own jewelry as she gave art and technology lectures. In those days, computers were boys' toys, and she felt it was important to dress up for her audiences. At the first lecture, Bonnie wore one of her crocheted collars with circuit boards. A woman waved her hand wildly during the question-and-answer period. The question was not about the intricacies of using a computer to make art but about where she might buy the same necklace. Bonnie sold it right off her neck; it certainly wouldn't be the last time she sold something while wearing it!

She still gives illustrated talks on art and technology but has added a lecture called "Crochet Ideas." A talk that fits both the technology category and falls into the purview of this book is "An Assistant in the Studio: How Textile Artists Use Computers." Bonnie has an MFA from the University of Washington in Seattle and has been exhibiting for

decades across the United States. Her artworks are in many private collections and a few public ones, including the National Science Foundation and the University of Washington. In the 1970s, her work appeared in numerous popular creative crochet books.

ANNE MONDRO received her BFA in crafts from the College for Creative Studies in Detroit, Michigan, in 1999, and completed her MFA in jewelry and metals at Kent State University in Ohio in 2002. Anne started crocheting with wire in 1998 after receiving Arline M. Fisch's book, *Textile Techniques in Metal*. With her mother's help, she first learned how to crochet with yarn, then began to explore working with wire. For her BFA exhibition, Anne created a series of crocheted necklaces composed of small repetitive forms.

Her recent crocheted necklaces continue to explore the idea of multiple elements. In these necklaces, colorful wire forms are highlighted with gold-filled wire for an elegant yet simple detail. The three-dimensional elements are then stitched together using wire.

Anne currently resides in Michigan and is a studio artist and instructor. In 2004, her work was displayed in the two-person show, *Keith Johnson and Anne Mondro: Photography and Silversmith Exhibition,* at Munson-Williams-Proctor Arts Institute in Utica, New York, and in an invitational exhibition titled *Fabrication* at Edinboro University of

Pennsylvania. Other exhibitions during 2003 included *bigLITTLE: Jewelers and Sculptors Making in Metal* at the Craft & Cultural Arts Gallery in Oakland, California; *Colorful Memories: A Show of Emotion* at the Brookfield Craft Center in Brookfield, Connecticut; and the *Sixth International Open* at Woman Made Gallery in Chicago.

ANASTACIA PESCE'S educational focus was jewelry and metalsmithing. She first earned a BFA at California College of the Arts (formerly California College of Arts and Crafts), then received an MA from San Diego State University. She noticed the technical similarities between the raising process, which requires the use of concentric rows of hammer blows, and the hook-and-wire row-building process of crochet. Each technique uses a similar concept of planning and turning rows into volumetric form. Raising is a slow and methodical process that requires a great deal of skill and patience to gently shape a flat disc into a three-dimensional form through repeated sequences of hammering and annealing. In contrast, the results in crochet are far more immediate, with the rows growing rapidly one loop at a time. Anastacia loves the value-added aesthetic of the by-product, unique to the crochet process, of the intrinsic textured surface created by cumulative stitches.

The properties of crochet add a new and exciting dimension to her technical vocabulary, enabling her to combine surface pattern and structure to express form. She enjoys the directness and simplicity of the materials and tools, and finds the quietness of the process to be quite therapeutic. She has, through practice and exploration, become remarkably fluent and comfortable with the crochet technique, able to manipulate the hook and wire to create simple and elegant forms with ease.

ZUZANA RUDAVSKA was born in Bratislava, Slovakia, where her early education was in fiber art at the University of Fine Arts and Crafts in Prague. She moved to New York City in 1986 and now lives in both the United States and Slovakia. Her experience and knowledge of traditional craftsmanship and her skill in various fiber techniques enabled her to begin experimenting with new materials and forms. This has led to an innovative use of wire in woven and crocheted structures, as well as more freehand structures in wire, sisal, jute, and stone. Since 1982, she has been combining copper, silver, and gold wire with various semiprecious crystals and other natural materials to create harmony and contrast. In addition to making one-of-a-kind jewelry, Zuzana works in a wide range of disciplines, including drawing, sculpture, mixed-media objects, and monumental site-specific installations. Her work in all media incorporates fiber elements by using fiber techniques and/or materials. She describes the process of designing

jewelry as similar to that of creating small sculpture. The necklace or bracelet becomes something upon which to meditate, something to hold in the hand and touch. With nature as her greatest inspiration, she creates work in the hope that pieces made of natural materials will reconnect the wearer with the environment.

Zuzana participates in exhibitions around the world, and had solo exhibitions in Slovakia in 2002 and 2004. She shows her work regularly in galleries in the United States and Europe, and her work has been published in many international catalogs, books, and magazines. She is represented in numerous public and private collections.

ANNEGRET SCHMID was born in Germany and received her degree in jewelry from the Fachhochschule für Gestaltung in Pforzheim, Germany, in 1997. Following her MFA, she worked as a designer for companies in both Switzerland and Germany. During that time, Annegret also worked as a jewelry instructor, teaching summer courses in 1999 at the Nova Scotia College of Art and Design in Halifax, Nova Scotia, Canada.

Since 1995, Annegret has worked in her own studio, exhibiting in Germany, Switzerland, Canada, and the United States. Her personal work is focused on memory jewelry, which historically includes wedding, friendship, and memento-mori pieces. The idea and the

concept, combined with thoughts or meaning from which the finished work evolves, are more significant for Annegret than simply creating a beautiful piece. That the work approaches her customers in an emotional and thoughtful way is also important. She wants it to interact with the viewer, encourage personal reflection, evoke feelings of happiness or sadness, and engender introspection.

LILO SERMOL has lived and studied in Germany, Austria, Chile, and the United States, pursuing a wide variety of art forms, from drawing and watercolor painting to fashion design, silk painting, and bead and metal jewelry. For years she has painted on silk to create wall hangings and one-of-a-kind wearable art pieces. Necklaces and earrings in beads and wire embellish the clothing and are an extension of the process of wearable art.

Lilo knits and crochets in a variety of wires, including fine silver and color-coated copper in brilliant colors. She incorporates beads and pearls into her wire constructions to add color and brilliance to her already exuberant compositions. She is concerned with balancing positive and negative space, and with the animation of line created by the nature of the wire she uses.

Her work has been showcased in gallery exhibitions in the United States, Germany, and Austria. She designs her wearable art for private clients but is also represented by galleries and shops on the West Coast.

MICHAEL DAVID STURLIN'S hand-crocheted gold necklaces have been featured in numerous jewelry magazines. Select jewelry and art galleries throughout the United States represent him, and Michael has received awards for his crochet work from the World Gold Council and the American Jewelry Design Council.

Raised by his grandparents on an Appaloosa horse ranch in Wyoming, he had regular chores to carry out, many involving crafts and handiwork. He learned to braid, crochet, knit, and do beadwork from his grandmother, who also taught him the value that comes from working quietly and diligently for long periods of time. He considers the crochet he now creates in gold wire to be a form of meditation, because it requires total concentration to accomplish without mishap.

Working exclusively in 18-karat gold in yellow, white, and red, Michael crochets elegant chains that flow fluidly around the neck and can be worn on their own, braided in multiples, or accompanied by pendants of precious gemstones. Self-taught as a goldsmith, he eventually refined his skills in stonesetting and metalwork at the Revere Academy of Jewelry Arts in San Francisco. He is married to a native of Thailand; while living there, he studied with Thai and Chinese goldsmiths.

Michael's method of crocheting is different because he doesn't work from a continuous source of wire, instead using shorter lengths that can be threaded through each loop to make additional loops. As his primary tool, he utilizes a needle set in a wooden handle instead of a crochet hook. He threads the wire through each loop with his fingers and then wraps it around the tool to form consistently sized loops. This produces an interlooping structure similar to that of spool knitting, but with greater control and density. The final step of annealing to relax the loops, then pulling the tubular structure through a drawplate to even out the diameter, is a challenging one, but essential to the perfection of the completed piece.

artist index

BEHRENS, HANNE, Nibe, Denmark, 29, 44, 86, 110, 117

BELL, EUGENIE KEEFER, Garran, Australia, 16, 25, 36, 109, 113, 114

DULLA, JOAN, Chandler, Arizona, 14, 26, 102, 110

FISCH, ARLINE M., San Diego, California, 6, 7, 21, 22, 32, 41, 46, 48, 68, 70, 93, 96, 98, 100, 112

HARRIS, KATHRYN, San Diego, California, 24, 80, 112

HAWLEY, KANDY, Orange, California, 19, 84

HOLDER, TINA FUNG, Washburn, Wisconsin, 29, 56, 109, 114, 116

KVAMMEN, INGER BLIX, Hesseng, Norway, 15, 34, 38, 108, 111, 117

MATHES, JESSE, Chicago, Illinois, 28, 90, 111, 115, 116

MELTZER, BONNIE, Portland, Oregon, 27, 76, 112

MONDRO, ANNE, Ann Arbor, Michigan, 11, 61, 114, 117

PESCE, ANASTACIA, Cambridge, New York, 20, 51, 54, 58, 109, 113

RUDAVSKA, ZUZANA, Brooklyn, New York, 17, 25, 78, 110, 112, 113, 115, 117

SCHMID, ANNEGRET, Pforzheim, Germany, 17, 64

SERMOL, LILO, Lake Oswego, Oregon, 18, 73, 111, 116

STURLIN, MICHAEL DAVID, Scottsdale, Arizona, 105, 109, 110, 113, 115

acknowledgments

I am indebted to the 15 artists who so generously gave of their time and talent to produce an exciting array of projects for this book. When I hesitantly asked for their participation, I never expected such enthusiastic responses. Each artist eagerly accepted the invitation to design and produce a project (in some cases more than one) along with detailed instructions. I suspect that the projects were the fun part, and the written instructions were a not-very-welcome task, quite beyond the usual parameters of those who make personal and unique works. I am most grateful for their contributions, and appreciative of the quality and variety of the projects developed specifically for this publication. Thank you all very much!